Group Techniques
for
Program Planning

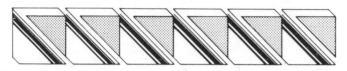

Management Applications Series

Alan C. Filley, University of Wisconsin, Madison
Series Editor

Performance in Organizations: Determinants and Appraisal
L. L. Cummings, University of Wisconsin, Madison
Donald P. Schwab, University of Wisconsin, Madison

Leadership and Effective Management
Fred E. Fiedler, University of Washington
Martin M. Chemers, University of Utah

Managing by Objectives
Anthony P. Raia, University of California, Los Angeles

Organizational Change: Techniques and Applications
Newton Margulies, University of California, Irvine
John C. Wallace, University of California, Irvine

Interpersonal Conflict Resolution
Alan C. Filley, University of Wisconsin, Madison

*Group Techniques for Program Planning: A Guide to Nominal
   Group and Delphi Processes*
Andre L. Delbecq, University of Wisconsin, Madison
Andrew H. Van de Ven, Kent State University
David H. Gustafson, University of Wisconsin, Madison

Organizational Behavior Modification
Fred Luthans, University of Nebraska, Lincoln
Robert Kreitner, Western Illinois University

Group Techniques
for
Program Planning

a guide to nominal group and delphi processes

Andre L. Delbecq
University of Wisconsin, Madison

Andrew H. Van de Ven
Kent State University

David H. Gustafson
University of Wisconsin, Madison

Scott, Foresman and Company • Glenview, Illinois
Dallas, Tex. • Oakland, N.J. • Palo Alto, Cal. • Tucker, Ga.

Library of Congress Catalog Number: 74-19717
ISBN: 0-673-07591-5

Foreword

The Management Applications Series is concerned with the application of contemporary research, theory, and techniques. There are many excellent books at advanced levels of knowledge, but there are few which address themselves to the application of such knowledge. The authors in this series are uniquely qualified for this purpose, since they are all scholars who have experience in implementing change in real organizations through the methods they write about.

Each book treats a single topic in depth. Where the choice is between presenting many approaches briefly or a single approach thoroughly, we have opted for the latter. Thus, after reading the book, the student or practitioner should know how to apply the methodology described.

Selection of topics for the series was guided by contemporary relevance to management practice, and by the availability of an author qualified as an expert, yet able to write at a basic level of understanding. No attempt is made to cover all management methods, nor is any sequence implied in the series, although the books do complement one another. For example, change methods might fit well with managing by objectives.

The books in this series may be used in several ways. They may be used to supplement textbooks in basic courses on management, organizational behavior, personnel, or industrial psychology/sociology. Students appreciate the fact that the material is immediately applicable. Practicing managers will want to use individual books to increase their skills, either through self study or in connection with management development programs, inside or outside the organization.

Alan C. Filley

Acknowledgments

The Nominal Group Technique (NGT) and the Delphi Technique are two group processes which the authors have utilized very successfully for program planning. Indeed, this book is our answer to the continuing flow of correspondence asking for more information about both techniques. This was not always the state of affairs. With reference to NGT, its development, application, and refinement is recent history. The technique was first tested in 1969. During that time, many administrators and planners were willing to work with us while the process was still experimental and our skills quite limited. It is only fair to acknowledge those organizations and individuals who were instrumental in the development of the knowledge underlying this book.

First, a debt of thanks to the Institute for Research in Poverty, and particularly Myron Lefcowitz, who provided the initial funding for research on NGT. Special thanks are extended to the Dane County Community Action Agency. Appreciation must also be given to Thomas Johns and Sue Simmons of Community Training and Development, Inc.

The Office of Comprehensive Health Planning, HEW, was a second major source of support. In particular, we would like to recognize Robert Brook and his staff, as well as Edward Van Ness and the late Richard Schlesinger. Sylvia Levy provided our first cross-cultural test by helping us prepare training programs in Hawaii and Micronesia. Dr. Alberta Parker initiated our exploration of applications for community health programs and primary care programs. Barbara Northrup greatly enhanced our understanding of the complex sociopolitical realities in comprehensive health planning. Many regional planning agencies of the Office of Housing and Urban Development have also been particularly helpful in providing opportunities for experiment and application. Particularly noteworthy has been the insight and feedback from Lorenz Aggens.

The Division of Student Affairs at the University of Wisconsin, Madison, provided the opportunity for refined empirical testing of NGT. The help of two people from that division, Marian Laines and Robert Ebersol, should be noted. At a time of cutbacks in University funding, their cooperation was much appreciated.

One of the most critical experiences in the development of our skills with nominal groups was the application of NGT in the Governor's Health Policy and Planning Task Force of the State of Wisconsin. Special thanks go to our colleagues in that experiment: David Carley, John Gregrich, Dr. Marc Hansen, Robert Meyers, and Sarah Dean.

Dr. C. Wesley Eisele has provided us with the opportunity to discuss and apply our techniques in the medical staff area. Dr. Eisele's continuing support has accounted for wide application of the techniques among medical staff personnel.

Of the many individuals in the early development of our experiences, however, two persons must be singled out. Without June Spencer of Opinion Research Associates, neither the opportunity to work with social and poverty agencies nor the feedback to improve our techniques would have been possible. Of all the administrators and planners we have encountered, she has been the greatest source of insight and assistance in applying the techniques to program planning. Finally, but not least, we must acknowledge the help of Roberta Wallace, who has been the key trainer and communicator of the techniques outside the author group, and whose help, warmth, and charm have carried tired scholars through many difficult meetings.

David Gustafson would like to acknowledge Dr. Murray Turoff of the Newark College of Engineering, who has had the most impact in helping develop applications of the Delphi Technique to program planning. Others playing a significant role in the Delphi Technique include Jerome Kaufman and Dr. Marc Hansen.

At this point, a host of other names and faces come to mind: administrators in health planning agencies, regional planning agencies, community action agencies, family service agencies, and hospitals, and many organizations whose friendship, assistance, patience, and cooperation stand behind this book. To all of our friends in these organizations, a sincere thanks for their help and patience.

Andre L. Delbecq
Andrew H. Van de Ven
David H. Gustafson

Introduction

  This is a book for practitioners in the human services—but "practice" widely interpreted. For it is a book that explains, lucidly and in detail, the Nominal Group Technique (NGT) and the Delphi Technique, tools that serve a broad variety of interests: those of the urban, health, or social planner; of the organizational manager; of the researcher generating a base for evaluation; of the educator seeking to enhance participation in the full development of particular issues; and of all who must accommodate policy decisions to diverse points of view and desires. Planner, manager, researcher, teacher, policy maker—all will find assistance in overcoming commonly encountered barriers occurring whenever groups face the task of defining problems and exploring solutions. These are methods designed to increase the creative productivity of group action, facilitate group decision, help stimulate the generation of critical ideas, give guidance in the aggregation of individual judgments and, in all these endeavors, save human effort and energy and leave participants with a sense of satisfaction.

  The authors remind us that management has its own "energy crisis": that as much as 80 percent of a chief administrator's day may be spent in committee meetings. We little need such reminders. The work that is never finished during the day and the bulging briefcase taken home at night are mute evidence of the paucity of time for quiet, undisrupted effort during the administrator's work day. More difficult to face, however, is the lack of resolution and sense of frustration that accompany so many committee and staff meetings. Group processes too often leave participants exhausted and discouraged because of the seemingly endless meanderings into unfruitful byways in what the authors refer to as "reactive search"; because of the focus effect that occurs when a group is unable to extricate itself from one channel of thought; or because of the mixing of solutions with problems and problems with solutions. What group has not had to face the tendency to develop solutions before problems are even delineated? Dominance by overtalkers? The suppression of disparate or conflicting ideas because of differences in power or authority, prestige, age, race, sex, or different levels of professionalization? What group has not experienced the general lack of creativity and absence of a sense of closure which leaves them with a feeling of impotence, boredom, and frustration, and the "well, nothing accomplished again!" syndrome? These problems, endemic in organizations, are costly in time and energy; the need for methods to overcome them is clear.

The Delphi Technique was created by Dalkey and his associates at the Rand Corporation in 1950. NGT was developed by Andre Delbecq and Andrew Van de Ven in 1968. Both techniques have already been widely employed in human service organizations—in education, health, and the social services. Also, both have been used increasingly as tools for evaluative research. The wide recognition given to NGT has occurred in a relatively short time, even with little documentation available in the literature. In my own field of health care, for example, it has been increasingly used although only one article has been published in a health-oriented journal. Starting with Andre Delbecq's own sorties into the world of human services—into community action agencies, comprehensive health and regional planning agencies, and neighborhood health centers—its use has diffused through an informal network of professionals. Those learning it under the authors' tutelage took it back and taught others; pupils became teachers, and in this manner knowledge has spread with a ripple effect in an ever-widening circle. Yet this type of diffusion, important as it is, has its limits. For wider dissemination, NGT needs an easily available and complete account of its use as well as its relationship to similar methods, such as the Delphi process.

This, then, is the authors' task. They carry it out in five tightly packed chapters. The first introduces the reader to the need for group methods to be used in "judgmental decision making." Here the authors emphasize that "judgmental decisions are facilitated by judgmental techniques" and that when this type of decision making is appropriate, groups must be prepared to jettison traditional meeting formats. The second chapter reviews the research on small group decision making and the constraints which the usual coordinative and information exchange meeting places on problem solving.

Chapters 3 and 4 provide explicit and detailed guidelines for NGT and the Delphi Technique. I have heard Professor Delbecq give an explanation of NGT on a number of occasions. I have sometimes wondered whether or not his facility in providing pithy illustrative examples and his own dynamic style make his personal appearance a necessary ingredient to effective understanding of the process. But this worry was unfounded. The technique is as clearly and convincingly explained in writing as it is when presented in person. By taking us step by step through the process—even providing sample wording for explanatory presentations—the authors ensure that anyone will be amply instructed and ready to employ these methods successfully in NGT meetings.

The final chapter discusses in detail the use of NGT in planning exploratory research, involving citizens, identifying multidisciplinary experts, and reviewing project proposals.

NGT IN HEALTH CARE ADMINISTRATION

Perhaps I was given the honor of writing this introduction because I happen to be one of a rapidly enlarging group of professional practitioners who have used NGT for a variety of purposes and in diverse settings. I feel comfortable in accepting this assignment even though I am not a theorist of organizations or of group process, because as a practitioner and teacher of health care administration I have been deeply impressed with what NGT can accomplish and with the ease and utility of its use. I have used it, or portions of it, in common administrative problem-solving situations. I have also used it to plan for a continuing education program for staff members and consumer boards of health centers. I have used it in graduate seminars in a school of public health and in consumer training programs. With Andre Delbecq, I used it to define problems facing comprehensive health planning boards in Hawaii, Guam, and six governmental districts of Micronesia (in the last setting the participants spoke many different languages and had to be assisted in the nominal process by translators). Most recently we employed NGT in a research project to develop consumer and professional definitions of the uniquely important roles and qualities of primary health care organizations. I can, therefore, fully attest to its advantages in planning, administration, continuing education, academic teaching, and research. My evaluation of its effectiveness is based on four types of evidence: (1) the greater flow of ideas I have seen generated when compared with traditional meetings; (2) the fuller participation of all those involved in contrast to other settings; (3) the increased evidence of the task being brought to closure; and (4) the evident sense of satisfaction on the part of participants about these three accomplishments.

Over time I have also been able to answer in large part the principal reservations I have had about its use. Will there be differences in participation between persons coming from different cultures or different socioeconomic backgrounds? Can diverse groups participate effectively together? Do participants feel manipulated, coerced, and resentful because of the rigidity of the process? Is a charismatic leader necessary to make it work? Can inappropriate use be avoided or minimized? In answer to these questions, I should like to share some of my observations.

In my experience, this technique seems to work in groups made up of members from any socioeconomic level or culture. We have used it successfully with members of poverty communities and also with some of the nation's leading experts on health care. We have used it with professors and persons with grade-school educations. We have used it with English-speaking participants and those needing translators. It has also proven to be effective and acceptable in groups where backgrounds are mixed and, as the authors point out, it allows what in other settings might be conflictual or potentially offending statements to be brought out, clarified, and ranked without strife or discord. It creates situations where those who might not participate for reasons inherent in ideology or in the social situation become full partners. In Guam, for example, the NGT groups contained Chamorran women from the villages who spoke little English alongside women from the capital city who were active in civic affairs. It became quite clear after the first few hours of the day that both groups took deep satisfaction in the work they accomplished. One of the Chamorran women told me afterward that she had had great fear of having to speak in what she considered her inadequate English. Soon, to her great surprise, she felt very comfortable in presenting the items on her list and in assisting in their clarification. Recently we went through a somewhat similar experience in a Southern city of the United States. The participants, while all Southerners, represented a particularly wide range in age, sex, race, and social status. The person most obviously under anticipatory tension in this group was a white woman of upper-class background. Her hands were clenched at the beginning. As the day wore on she relaxed; soon her participation was enthusiastic.

Questions about the rigidity of the process and whether or not it will be perceived as manipulation or coercion must be given serious consideration. In my experience, no matter the background (and we have used it with groups whose members were particularly sensitive to being manipulated), participants have *not* resented the structure. But —and I feel that this is a critical point—we have *always* had skilled leaders to explain the rationale and guide the process. In clumsy or insensitive hands, or in the clutch of someone who wished to exploit rigidity for purposes of control, the results might well be otherwise.

This cautionary note raises the issue of the quality of leadership and its importance to the success or failure of the NGT process. The quality of leadership *is* of great importance. It requires not only someone who feels comfortable with all phases of the process, but one who can also provide understandable and reasonable explanations and who possesses sensitivity to unasked questions. It requires someone who has the ability to impose structure in a nonthreatening manner and, during the clarification period, someone who is able to move the discussion along briskly, keep it from becoming bogged down in detailed anecdotes or "position papers," and at the same time avoid hurting anyone's feelings. These tasks obviously cannot be accomplished by everyone.

This brings me to its appropriate use. NGT can be and has been used in a variety of settings. For example, in the next section, Angelo Fortuna of ARA Services, Inc., discusses its applications in a business setting. The authors stress, however, that NGT is not a panacea to overcome all problems of small group process; it must be used with discrimination. Because of the necessity for preplanning, for adherence to a predetermined procedural structure, and for an adequate amount of time, it cannot be used in the average meeting. Additionally, the effort required on the part of the participants goes far beyond passive attendance. For these reasons, it should not be considered for routine decision making. Its use is for issues adjudged especially important, where it is essential to have wide and representative input, and where difficulties in ranking and rating problems or solutions as a basis for group decisions are such that the traditional meeting is of relatively little use.

Alberta W. Parker, M.D.
Clinical Professor of
    Community Health
School of Public Health
University of California, Berkeley

NGT IN A BUSINESS SETTING

Since Dr. Parker's presentation has previewed the excellence and format of the book and provided expert testimony as to the value of the techniques and the clarity with which they are presented, I would like to focus on applications of the techniques to my organization, ARA Services, Inc.

We have used NGT in many parts of the corporation to which I belong, under various circumstances, in the face of very real difficult situations, and with a wide variety of leaders. Never once has it failed us. On the other hand, although I was introduced to the Delphi Technique while serving in the Air Force, I have not attempted its implementation with my present corporate structure. (We have, however, used a modified Delphi, coupling the computer and a convened group for instructional purposes.) Thus my remarks will, like those of Dr. Parker, emphasize the use of NGT.

The need for careful planning and the distributed effort required by the Delphi Technique limits its use in normal business operations. In testimonial to this book, however, I find that the Delphi Technique is so clearly explained that I shall attempt its use in the preparation of a performance evaluation system, with inputs from the geographically dispersed personnel managers in our organization. My guess is that as a result of the authors' presentation of the Delphi Technique more frequent use will be made of the tool in the business community. It certainly provides the opportunity for those back at the corporate headquarters to accomplish meaningful goals over a period of time, using the vast resources of an organization without requiring the convocation of a group and the attendant expense of traveling.

Our first use of NGT was in its classical application both as a problem-identification and problem-solving process. This first application occurred in August of 1971 during the reorganization of a major portion of the Food Services Company. A recounting of the use of the technique during the reorganization of the company should serve to reveal its varied expressions.

A decision was made by top management to focus on the human problems associated with the major reorganization and with the change from an essentially national, "product" marketing organization to one in which the several services were integrated within a geographical area. When the degree of anxiety of the participants of the first meeting (June 1971) revealed that truth in management was not necessarily credible, those attending were split off into small groups led by team monitors. I developed a team monitor approach for that meeting from ideas generated by the work of Maier and Solem reported in 1952. Although that technique served our situation quite well, it was dependent on the training of local behavioral scientists to act as team monitors. To gain foothold in the organization, the approach would have required extensive training of the individual practitioner/manager. Fortunately, an article on NGT by Professors Van de Ven and Delbecq was published in the June 1971 issue of the *Academy of Management Journal,* and I was able to read it prior to the follow-up meeting held in August. By using NGT at the August meeting we were able to elicit concerns regarding organizational and personal problems and determine further communications required from the assembled managers, in a very cost-effective manner. We called it "peeling the group of concerns." The technique was then used in a more classical sense to generate alternatives for the solution of specific problems that had been surfaced by the "peeling." Although we did not attempt a methodological study to determine the effectiveness of the technique, the number of issues that surfaced and the quality of the solutions that were suggested indicated that NGT was a powerful technique. While it is not possible to assess the impact of its use on the company reorganization, it is noteworthy that we were able to accomplish the entire restructuring in one year instead of the predicted two, without a slowdown in the growth of sales volume or revenue and with a lower turnover of managerial personnel than had occurred prior to that time.

A novel use of the technique was as a process to establish the identity of new leaders in the changed organization. The persons who were selected to head the subdivisions of the organization were trained in NGT prior to the meeting. During the meeting, people were shifted from the organizational unit to which they had previously belonged to their new organizational units and placed in an NGT group, with the new head of their unit acting as the leader of the group. We believed that this would be an ideal leadership situation; the NGT leader was providing direction toward accomplishing a goal, and because of his nonpunitive role, was being fully considerate of the feelings of others. Our experience justified this belief.

To summarize, we were able to make effective use of NGT for identifying problems, improving problem solving, and establishing leadership roles during a major reorganization program. As an outgrowth of this meeting, the technique was later adapted by the Vice President of Sales of the Prototype Area. He found it to be a most useful device for capturing ideas from all of the sales personnel while at the same time minimizing the rejection of ideas that normally occurred in interacting meetings.

The most dramatic use of the technique I have experienced was by the Vice President of Sales of the Central Area. During a very hectic meeting in which there appeared to be no attention to any task, he wanted to solicit concerns of the individuals about changes in organization and economic pressures. He turned to me and asked, "Should we try NGT?" My response was, "I don't think it will work but try it anyway." He then gave the instructions for the technique (most of the sales group had already had prior experience with it) and started the quiet writing. Immediately, the group turned to the task and the round-robin elicitation produced fifty-five items to which he later responded.

Chapter 3 of this book, which explains NGT in detail, represents a wealth of understanding that deserves the full attention of even the most experienced NGT leader. Although the basic value of the chapter is for training people in NGT, there is something in it for all of us. To that same end, I would like to contribute some random observations emanating from the use of the technique:

1) The seeming simplicity of the technique is deceptive. An experiential process for training in its use is suggested.

2) The crispness of the technique and the lack of social interaction conflicts with social needs that are often part of the organizational conference meeting or group session. Participants should be prepared to commit themselves to action before attempting to use NGT to address problems.

3) The experience in our organization shows that, in identifying problems, organizational problems are most quickly elicited. Only later are personal problems of major import verbalized.

4) Some participants appear better able to generate ideas during the round-robin period than during the period of quiet writing. Therefore, it is important that each person be addressed in turn even after they have passed for a single round.

5) Valid contributions are easily solicited from personnel who are normally noted for their quietness and reticence to advance data in group sessions.

6) To the degree that the NGT leader/recorder is openly receptive to inputs from the group during the round-robin period, trust seems to be developed quickly.

In reviewing what I have written, it is apparent that there is the predicted disproportionate emphasis on NGT as opposed to the Delphi Technique. This should not be perceived as depreciating the value of the Delphi Technique under appropriate circumstances. I have attempted here to share my experience as an active practitioner in business with those of you who are learning about the techniques through the medium of this excellent book. Finally, I am certainly enamored of the techniques and owe a great and real debt to the authors. Where the alchemists failed in their search for a way to transmute base to noble metals, the authors have succeeded in developing a process to convert leaden group sessions into golden opportunities for problem resolution.

Angelo L. Fortuna
Director of Manpower and Organization
   Development
ARA Services, Inc.

Contents

Group Decision Making in Modern Organizations

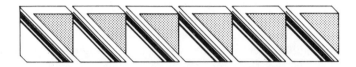

Increasingly, practicing administrators or professionals are seeking useful new techniques to increase rationality, creativity, and participation in problem-solving meetings associated with program planning. As the number of occasions requiring pooled judgments in planning increases, so does the need for increased skill in conducting such meetings.

In this volume we shall focus on two specific techniques: the Delbecq and Van de Ven Nominal Group Technique (NGT), and the Delphi Technique. At the completion of the book, the practicing administrator or professional planner should thoroughly understand the theory, research, and practical problems surrounding both methodologies. When properly utilized and applied, both techniques are powerful tools for increasing a group's creative capacity to generate critical ideas and understand problems and the component parts of their solutions; thus, participants can aggregate (pool) individual judgments and arrive at desirable group decisions.

THE NATURE OF PROGRAM PLANNING

Program as we are using the term implies a prearranged set of activities which specify the means to achieve a goal. In the public sector (health, education, welfare, and government), a program is formulated in order to provide services which accomplish defined human service objectives. For example, a crisis intervention program specifies technical and professional activities aimed at ameliorating personal suffering, preventing suicides, and providing comfort to individuals facing personal crises. In the private sector (business and industry), a program may refer to a set of technological manipulations required to manufacture a product. In summary, a program is the means-end sequence necessary to provide a specific service or product.

Program planning is the process underlying the development or modification of programs. Administrators and professional planners are increasingly being asked to participate in special committees, task-force groups, or technical teams concerned with recommending new programs or changing existing programs. Where the changes in programs or the development of new programs occur under complex circumstances, the participants face real challenges.

Conditions which lead to complexity in program planning would include the following situations, familiar to every program administrator or professional planner (Brief, Delbecq, and Filley, 1974; Delbecq, 1974): [1]

1) There is low organizational readiness to adopt the new program due to:
   a. limited awareness of the importance of client problems which the program proposal addresses.
   b. limited understanding of available solutions due to either lack of modeling by earlier organizations who have adopted similar programs, or lack of codified and agreed-upon scientific or technical models and lack of experimental evidence.

2) A large number of individuals or groups (e.g., providers, clients, funders, professionals, and administrators) constitute the decision set which will have to approve the program and which will review the proposal under conditions where:
   a. the groups have different value and conceptual orientations.
   b. prior communication networks based on joint participation in the development of earlier successful programs do not exist.

1. *These two papers are concerned with detailed theoretical and empirical elaborations of the sociopolitical complexities of program planning.*

3) The proposed program will have a great impact on present organizational arrangements and allocation of resources due to:
    a. limited slack resources.
    b. absence of major outside funding.

Appropriate program-planning processes must be adopted to cope with these complex planning situations. Fortunately, there is high agreement concerning the general sequence of steps which planners must follow in such cases. The authors have developed a model of sequential planning steps called PPM (Program Planning Model) which suggests that critical features of program planning under conditions of complexity should include (Delbecq and Van de Ven, 1971; Van de Ven and Delbecq, 1972):

- Obtaining early review of the planning intent, and a clear mandate from top-level decision makers concerning the general approach followed in developing the program.
- Involving clients or consumers in problem exploration meetings to document unmet needs.
- Involving outside resource people (both scientific and technical) to help explore components of an appropriate program to solve those needs.
- Involving administrators, funding sources, clients, and professionals in an early review of program plans.
- Involving appropriate personnel in developing designs for implementation and evaluation.
- Involving other personnel, from organizations who will be later adopters of the new program, as participant observers in a demonstration program, to prepare the way for technological transfer or diffusion of innovative programs.

GROUP TECHNIQUES AND PROGRAM PLANNING

In this book, we will focus upon group techniques useful in program planning and administration. Obviously many other elements enter into program planning beyond group meetings. Nonetheless, since key processes include: (1) problem exploration; (2) knowledge exploration; (3) preliminary review; (4) design and implementation teams; and (5) evaluation and review meetings; then group processes which facilitate the sharing of judgments at each of these critical junctures are important.

Since NGT and the Delphi Technique are but two specific types of group processes, it is important to differentiate them from other group processes such as bargaining, confrontation, hearings, etc., which also have their places in program administration and planning.

The nature of NGT and the Delphi Technique

Like other group techniques (e.g., force-field analysis and parliamentary procedure), NGT and the Delphi Technique are not a panacea for all group meetings. They are special-purpose techniques useful for situations where individual judgments must be tapped and combined to arrive at decisions which cannot be calculated by one person. They are problem-solving or idea-generating strategies, not techniques for routine meetings, coordination, bargaining, or negotiations.

Since the distinction between judgmental versus other types of meeting situations is an important distinction, a word of elaboration is worthwhile so the reader clearly understands the type of meeting we are concerned with in this book.

We are not concerned with *routine* meetings. Generally speaking, we can define a routine meeting as a situation where members of the group agree upon the desired goal, and technologies exist to achieve this goal.[2] In such a meeting the focus is on coordination and information exchange, and the meeting is "leader-centered" (Delbecq, 1967). In a program-planning situation, this task would be delegated to a trained technical expert or team of experts to handle based on established formulas.

Likewise, we are not concerned with *negotiation* or *bargaining*. We can define this situation as one in which opposing factions differing in norms, values, or vested interests stand in opposition to each other concerning either ends, means, or both. The management of conflict and the formulation of *representative* groups is also outside our focus

2. In Simon's terminology, this is the "programmed" decision situation (Simon, 1960); in Thompson's terminology, this is the "computational" decision situation (Thompson, 1959).

(Delbecq, 1967). In a program-planning context, this situation occurs when opposing factions have assumed hardened positions based on strong value differences.

We *are* concerned with *judgmental* decision making.[3] Colloquially, we are talking about *creative* decision making. The central element of this situation is the lack of agreement or incomplete state of knowledge concerning either the nature of the problem or the components which must be included in a successful solution. As a result, heterogeneous group members must pool their judgments to invent or discover a satisfactory course of action. Obviously, judgmental problem and solution exploration is but a subset of meetings important to administrators and planners in program planning. Nonetheless, the need for creative or judgmental problem solving occurs frequently. NGT and the Delphi Technique, along with other meeting formats, are important components in the repertoire of professional and managerial group skills which planners will find useful.

The increased need for pooled judgments

With growing frequency, then, contemporary program administrators or professional planners face situations where they must elicit and combine judgments in group meetings. Not only do administrators or planners need to involve their own professional staffs in program planning, but they are also often urged to find viable methods for tapping the judgments of various outside groups (e.g., resource experts, customers, clients, etc.) from different backgrounds, positions, and perspectives.

Unfortunately, organizational life for many administrators and professional planners has become an endless stream of committee meetings absorbing countless precious working hours. Indeed, a recurring complaint among administrators and planners is that they lack the time and opportunity to work alone and uninterrupted. It has been found that as much as 80 percent of a program administrator's working time is spent in committee meetings (Van de Ven, 1973). Simply on the basis of costs per working hour, it behooves the administrator or professional planner to explore more expedient, efficient processes for group decision making.

3. *Here we are talking about the situation which in Simon's terminology is "heuristic" and in Thompson's terminology is "judgmental."*

More important, however, is the fact that judgmental decisions are often obtained by utilizing the same group processes that dominate routine coordination and information exchange (Delbecq, 1963). It is a critical requirement of effective leadership, therefore, to redefine group roles and processes so that *judgmental decisions* are facilitated by *judgmental techniques*. This book will help the planner or administrator structure such judgmental situations away from the leader-centered coordination format of routine meetings.

This is an age of "maximum feasible participation" wherein client, user, or consumer groups in public and private organizations wish to participate in program planning and administration. In the public sector, citizen or client participation is often legally required in programs funded by federal agencies in health, education, welfare, and urban affairs. Such participation, however, is not restricted to the public sector, and the appropriateness of having administrators or professionals unilaterally plan or make decisions for customers has been questioned.

Yet, the involvement of user groups presents a dilemma for the organization striving to achieve maximum feasible participation. When both professional and client members are present within problem-solving groups, destructive dominance or confrontation is not unusual. Administrators who traditionally have been exposed only to comfortable interaction with homogeneous professional groups generally do not possess the skills to vitally and constructively involve lay personnel in meetings with staff or professional members. It has been claimed by D. P. Moynihan (1969) that client involvement using conventional group techniques has resulted in "maximum feasible misunderstanding." As a result, NGT in particular has been widely adopted as a method for client involvement in problem identification.

Citizen participation is not the only reason for increased group decision making. Another important force is the need to share expertise. Often, a particular professional does not command sufficient technological expertise to unilaterally develop solutions to complex problems. As the accumulation and specialization of knowledge increases, viable solutions to complex problems require the involvement of resource experts from heterogeneous disciplines or functions. This fact partly explains the proliferation of *ad hoc* problem-solving groups as opposed to standing committees in complex organizations.

Contemporary administrators repeatedly complain how difficult it is to develop effective dialogue among multifunctional or multidisciplinary resource personnel so that a new and creative frame of analysis can be brought to bear on a particular problem (Delbecq,

Van de Ven, and Wallace, 1972). As a result, at the end of a problem-solving meeting the administrator frequently leaves a conference feeling seduced by the "mind set" or framework of one or two assertive group members. Such meetings do not provide for adequate consideration of all facets of the problem or alternative solutions, because the cost of long meetings and the further availability of resource personnel makes further interaction impossible. Indeed, methods to quickly phase in outside personnel without becoming trapped in an exorbitant number of meetings are in short supply. The techniques treated in this book are specifically designed for such situations.

In summary, this volume is written for the program administrator or professional planner who must facilitate judgmental group meetings in settings such as those just discussed. It is directed toward answering the following specific questions:

1) How can I use NGT and the Delphi Technique to obtain group judgments?

2) Which technique should be used for what types of problems?

3) What skills and prerequisites are needed to implement each technique?

4) When real world constraints for calling group meetings (e.g., time, cost, and travel) become important considerations, how does one weigh the costs and benefits of choosing one technique over another?

THE NOMINAL GROUP TECHNIQUE

NGT [4] was developed by Andre L. Delbecq and Andrew H. Van de Ven in 1968. It was derived from social-psychological studies of

4. The term "nominal" was adopted by earlier researchers to refer to processes which bring individuals together but do not allow the individuals to communicate verbally. Thus, the collection of individuals is a group "in name only," or "nominally," since verbal exchange, a sine qua non for group behavior, is excluded. NGT combines both non-verbal and verbal stages, as will be elaborated in the text. Thus, NGT is more than a "nominal" group. Many researchers use a nominal process in differing formats, particularly emphasizing the generation of ideas as opposed to the generation, discussion, and mathematical evaluation format which is the normative process set forth by Delbecq and Van de Ven. For a review of other literature on nominal formats, refer to Van de Ven and Delbecq, 1971.

decision conferences, management-science studies of aggregating group judgments, and social-work studies of problems surrounding citizen participation in program planning. Since that time, NGT has gained extensive recognition and has been widely applied in health, social service, education, industry, and government organizations.

NGT is a structured group meeting which proceeds along the following format. Imagine a meeting room in which seven to ten individuals are sitting around a table in full view of each other; however, at the beginning of the meeting they do not speak to each other. Instead, each individual is writing ideas on a pad of paper in front of him or her. At the end of five to ten minutes, a structured sharing of ideas takes place. Each individual, in round-robin fashion, presents one idea from his or her private list. A recorder writes that idea on a flip chart in full view of other members. There is still no discussion at this point of the meeting—only the recording of privately narrated ideas. Round-robin listing continues until all members indicate they have no further ideas to share.

The output of this nominal phase of the meeting is a list of propositional statements usually numbering eighteen to twenty-five. Discussion follows during the next phase of the meeting; however, it is structured so that each idea receives attention before independent voting. This is accomplished by asking for clarification, or stating support or nonsupport of each idea listed on the flip chart. Independent voting then takes place. Each member privately, in writing, selects priorities by rank-ordering (or rating). The group decision is the mathematically pooled outcome of the individual votes.

To summarize, the process of decision making in NGT is as follows:

1) Silent generation of ideas in writing.

2) Round-robin feedback from group members to record each idea in a terse phrase on a flip chart.

3) Discussion of each recorded idea for clarification and evaluation.

4) Individual voting on priority ideas with the group decision being mathematically derived through rank-ordering or rating.

Thus, NGT overcomes a number of critical problems typical of interacting groups. (These problems will be discussed in Chapter 2.) For the moment, however, objectives of the process can be stated as follows:

GROUP DECISION MAKING IN MODERN ORGANIZATIONS 9

1) To assure different processes for each phase of creativity.

2) To balance participation among members.

3) To incorporate mathematical voting techniques in the aggregation of group judgment.

A brief word about each objective might be useful in this introductory description. As will be discussed in Chapter 2 when we review related small-group research, it is possible to identify two unique phases of creative or judgmental problem solving: a fact-finding phase and an evaluation phase. The fact-finding phase deals with problem search and the generation of data about the problem or, alternatively, about different proposed solutions. The evaluation phase is concerned with information synthesis, screening, and choosing among strategic elements of a problem or component elements of alternative solutions. There appears to be a consensus in research findings that these phases of problem solving are two distinct decision-making activities and require different roles and processes (Bales and Strodtbeck, 1969; Simon and Newell, 1958). In fact, to avoid group ambiguity about differences in decision-making phases, Maier and Hoffman (1964) suggest that one type of group process should be used to generate information and another type used to reach a solution.

The program administrator or planner should be concerned about which group decision-making process is appropriate in each phase of problem solving. For example, while a number of small-group theorists and practitioners question the viability of group interaction for the problem-identification or fact-finding phase, this does not imply that interaction is not appropriate for clarification and evaluation. Indeed, research by Vroom and his associates (1969) suggests that discussion is useful for evaluating, screening, and synthesizing phases of problem solving. A major advantage of the two techniques discussed in this book is that both NGT and the Delphi Technique involve different group processes for the phases of independent idea generation, structured feedback, and independent mathematical judgment (Gustafson, Shukla, Delbecq, and Walster, 1973).

A second advantage of the NGT format is the increased attention to each idea and increased opportunity for each individual to assure that his or her ideas are part of the group's frame of reference. The nominal (silent and independent) generation of ideas, the round-robin listing and serial discussion, and the independent voting all increase individual participation. By contrast, the conventional interacting group discussion generally succumbs to the influence of a few individuals due to status, personality, and other forces which we will thoroughly explore in Chapter 2.

Finally, the voting procedures in both techniques incorporate insights from mathematics and management science. Studies in these traditions have shown that the addition of simple mathematical voting procedures can greatly reduce errors in aggregating individual judgments into group decisions (Huber and Delbecq, 1972).

THE DELPHI TECHNIQUE[5]

Unlike the typical interacting meeting or NGT, where close physical proximity of group members is required for decision making, the Delphi Technique does not require that participants meet face to face. The Delphi Technique is a method for the systematic solicitation and collation of judgments on a particular topic through a set of carefully designed sequential questionnaires interspersed with summarized information and feedback of opinions derived from earlier responses.

To conduct the Delphi process, Turoff (1970) suggests at least three separate groups of individuals that perform three different roles:

Decision maker(s). The individual or individuals expecting some sort of product from the exercise which is used for their purposes.

A staff group. The group which designs the initial questionnaire, summarizes the returns, and redesigns the follow-up questionnaires.

A respondent group. The group whose judgments are being sought and who are asked to respond to the questionnaires.

The Delphi process was developed by Dalkey and his associates at the Rand Corporation. It has gained considerable recognition and is used in planning settings to achieve a number of objectives:

1) To determine or develop a range of possible program alternatives.

5. *The derivation of the label "Delphi" relates to the "Delphic Oracle." Delphi was originally used to forecast technological developments; thus, like the oracle, it was used to look into the future.*

2) To explore or expose underlying assumptions or information leading to different judgments.

3) To seek out information which may generate a consensus on the part of the respondent group.

4) To correlate informed judgments on a topic spanning a wide range of disciplines.

5) To educate the respondent group as to the diverse and interrelated aspects of the topic.

Although there appears to be agreement among practitioners on the above description of Delphi objectives, considerable variance is possible in Delphi formats relative to design and implementation. In particular, variations among practitioners in the administration of the Delphi Technique revolve around the following issues:

1) Whether the respondent group is anonymous.

2) Whether open-ended or structured questions are used to obtain information from the respondent group.

3) How many iterations of questionnaires and feedback reports are needed.

4) What decision rules are used to aggregate the judgments of the respondent group.

As we shall discuss in Chapter 4, which reviews the Delphi Technique in detail, the specific form of a Delphi is generally determined by the nature of the problem being investigated and constrained by the amount of human and physical resources available.

The basic approach used to conduct a Delphi can be exemplified, however, by a simplified Delphi situation wherein only two iterations of questionnaires and feedback are used. First, the staff team in collaboration with decision makers develops an initial questionnaire and distributes it by mail to the respondent group. The respondents independently generate their ideas in answer to the first questionnaire and return it. The staff team then summarizes the responses to the first questionnaire and develops a feedback report along with the second set of questionnaires for the respondent group. Having received the feedback report, the respondents independently evaluate earlier responses. Respondents are asked to independently vote on priority ideas included in the second questionnaire and mail their responses back to the staff team. The staff team then develops a final summary and feedback report to the respondent group and decision makers.

CHOOSING A DECISION-MAKING
PROCESS

Of course, the program manager's or planner's choice of a decision-making process will reflect real-world constraints, such as the number of working hours required for group decision making, the cost of utilizing committees, and the proximity of group participants. The Delphi process requires the least amount of time for participants. However, the calendar time required to obtain judgments from respondents may take significantly longer than NGT meetings. In addition, the staff time and cost to design and monitor the Delphi process may be more than the time and cost required to conduct an NGT or interacting meeting.

Physical proximity may also be a real world constraint affecting the practitioner's choice of a decision-making process. The Delphi Technique does not require participants to meet face to face, while NGT and interacting processes require physical proximity. However, if disagreements or conflicting perspectives need to be resolved, the practitioner may question the viability of the Delphi Technique, which uses a simple pooling of individual judgments without verbal clarification or discussion to resolve the differences.

In summary, concomitant with the advantages of a particular method for group decision making, there is also a need to know the cost associated with each process. In the final analysis, a comparative evaluation of the benefits and costs of NGT and the Delphi Technique may force the administrator to adopt a less than optimal technique for a given decision-making situation. These trade-offs will be discussed in some detail in Chapter 2.

LOOKING AHEAD

This book, then, is concerned with acquainting program administrators and planners with two relatively new group techniques for creative or judgmental problem solving: NGT and the Delphi Technique. Both techniques are capable of avoiding many difficulties encountered in the usual interacting group discussions so often used for judgmental problem solving.

In Chapter 2, we will examine in detail the theoretical and

empirical studies supporting the value of NGT and the Delphi Technique as opposed to interacting committee meetings. Those readers who are only interested in a detailed description of Delphi and NGT processes and benefits of both techniques, rather than the theoretical basis for the group processes, may wish to skip Chapter 2, which is somewhat complex, and turn directly to Chapters 3 and 4.

Chapter 3 is a training guide to utilizing NGT as a program-planning tool. Chapter 4 is a guide to utilizing the Delphi Technique. Chapter 5 discusses applications of NGT to typical program-planning situations: exploratory research, citizen participation, utilization of multidisciplinary experts, and proposal review. Although Chapter 5 focuses upon NGT, readers of Chapters 2 and 4 will easily see the opportunities to substitute the Delphi Technique for NGT, and will understand the conditions under which it is advantageous to do so.

REFERENCES

Bales, R. F., and F. L. Strodtbeck. "Phases in Group Problem Solving." In *Organizational Decision Making*. M. Alexis and C. Z. Wilson, eds., pp. 122–33. Prentice-Hall, 1969.

Brief, Arthur Paul, A. L. Delbecq, and A. C. Filley. "An Empirical Analysis of Adoption Behavior." Paper presented at the Academy of Management Annual Meeting, Seattle, Washington, 1974.

Delbecq, A. L. "Leadership in Business Decision Conferences." Doctoral dissertation, Indiana University Graduate School of Business, 1963.

Delbecq, A. L. "The Management of Decision Making Within the Firm: Three Strategies for Three Types of Decision Making." *Academy of Management Journal*, 10, 4 (December 1967): 329–39.

Delbecq, A. L. "Contextual Variables Affecting Decision Making in Program Planning." *Decision Sciences* (October 1974).

Delbecq, A. L., and A. H. Van de Ven. "A Group Process Model for Problem Identification and Program Planning." *Journal of Applied Behavioral Science* (July–August 1971).

Delbecq, A. L., A. H. Van de Ven, and R. Wallace. "Critical Problems in Health Planning: Potential Management Contributions."

Paper presented at 32nd Annual Meeting of Academy of Management, August 13–16, 1972.

Gustafson, David H., Ramesh K. Shukla, A. L. Delbecq, and G. William Walster. "A Comparative Study of Differences in Subjective Likelihood Estimates Made by Individuals, Interacting Groups, Delphi Groups, and Nominal Groups." *Organizational Behavior and Human Performance,* 9 (1973): 280–91.

Huber, George, and A. L. Delbecq. "Guidelines for Combining the Judgment of Individual Members in Decision Conferences." *Academy of Management Journal,* 15, 2 (June 1972): 161–74.

Maier, N. R. F., and L. R. Hoffman. "Quality of First and Second Solution in Group Problem Solving." *Journal of Applied Psychology,* 41 (1964): 320–23.

Moynihan, D. P. *Maximum Feasible Misunderstanding: Community Action in the War on Poverty.* Free Press, 1969.

Simon, Herbert A. *The New Science of Management Decisions,* Chapters 2 and 3. Harper Brothers, 1960.

Simon, Herbert A., and Allen Newell. "Heuristic Problem Solving: The Next Advance in Operations Research." *Operations Research Journal* (January–February 1958). Thompson and Tuden, cit.

Thompson, J., and Arthur Tuden. "Strategies, Structures, and Processes of Organizational Decisions." In *Comparative Studies in Administration.* Thompson et al., eds., pp. 198–99. University of Pittsburgh Press, 1959.

Turoff, M. "The Design of a Policy Delphi." *Technological Forecasting and Social Change,* 2 (1970).

Van de Ven, A. H. *An Applied Experimental Text of Alternative Decision-Making Processes.* Center for Business and Economic Research Press, Kent State University, 1973.

Van de Ven, A. H., and A. L. Delbecq. "Nominal versus Interacting Group Processes for Committee Decision-Making Effectiveness." *Academy of Management Journal* (June 1971).

Van de Ven, A. H., and A. L. Delbecq. "A Planning Process for Development of Complex Regional Programs." *Proceedings of the American Sociological Association Annual Meeting,* August, 1972.

Vroom, V. H., L. D. Grant, and T. J. Cotton. "The Consequences of Social Interaction in Group Problem Solving." *Journal of Applied Psychology,* 53, 4 (August 1969): 338–41.

Profile of
Small Group
Decision Making

2

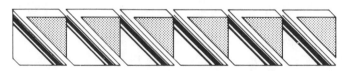

Our scientific knowledge of small group decision-making processes is incomplete. Nevertheless, a significant body of empirical knowledge exists that can provide the practitioner with general guidelines for structuring group decision-making processes for different types of problems. In particular, a number of research studies have examined the effects of alternative processes on the performance of decision-making groups in terms of (1) the quantity, quality, and variety of ideas generated; (2) the affectional (emotional and expressive) overtones of interaction; and (3) the nature of facilitative and inhibitive influences on creative problem solving. This chapter[1] will attempt to summarize the research by comparing the relative effectiveness of interacting,[2] nominal, and Delphi decision-making processes.

1. *The material in this chapter draws heavily from Van de Ven, 1974.*
2. *"Interacting" in the context of this chapter refers to a conventional discussion group format, which is generally an unstructured, free-flowing meeting, with minimal direction by the leader other than the presentation of the issue to the group. Obviously, a trained leader can create increasing degrees of structure in a discussion group, so that an interacting group can approximate a structured group process. However, one should then read "interacting" in this chapter as "unstructured discussion group."*

15

INTERACTING VERSUS
NOMINAL PROCESSES

The past fifteen years have seen a rapid growth of interest in the comparative effectiveness of individuals versus groups, and nominal versus interacting group methods in decision situations that require individuals to generate information concerning a problem. Osborn (1957), a major proponent of "brainstorming" techniques in problem solving, posited "the average person can think up twice as many ideas when working with a group than working alone." When comparing the average number of ideas produced by groups with the average number of ideas produced by individuals, brainstorming groups were found superior to an equal number of individuals brainstorming independently (Hall, Mouton, and Blake, 1963; Osborn, 1957). Further, brainstorming groups were found superior to conventional discussion groups in problem-solving situations (Bouchard, 1969; Osborn, 1957; Parnes and Meadow, 1959). Taylor, Berry, and Block (1958) found interacting groups superior to individuals in problem-solving situations when comparing the performance of individuals working alone with that of a group in which the same individuals participate at another time. They state: "Such group superiority may very well account for the widespread impression that group participation does facilitate the production of ideas."

Since the pioneering work of Osborn, various modifications have been made on the brainstorming technique. The method receiving the greatest research interest has been the *nominal group process,* where people work in the presence of each other but write ideas independently rather than talk about them. Three measures have generally been used to compare the relative effectiveness of nominal versus interacting group processes: (1) the average number of unique ideas; (2) the average total number of ideas; and (3) the quality of ideas produced.

In terms of these three measures of performance, nominal groups have been found to be significantly superior to interacting groups in generating information relevant to a problem (Bouchard, 1969; Bouchard and Hare, 1970; Campbell, 1968; Dunnette, Campbell, and Jaastad, 1963; Leader, 1963; Taylor et al., 1958; Vroom, Grant, and Cotton, 1969). Researchers have concluded that when the group task is to generate information on a problem, interacting groups inhibit creative thinking. (This is not a generic statement of superiority. For other purposes, such as attitude change, team building, and consensus generation, interacting groups are superior. The emphasis here is on *idea generation*.) Individual inhibitions and premature evaluation in interacting groups result in a decrease in quality of group ideas in terms of creativity, originality, and practicality (Collaros and Anderson, 1969). A focus effect is also characteristic of interacting groups; that is, the group tends to pursue a single train of thought for long periods (Dunnette et al., 1963; Taylor et al., 1958).

NGT VERSUS
THE DELPHI TECHNIQUE

A comparison of the decision-making steps in NGT and the Delphi Technique, outlined in Chapter 1, suggests that the two techniques are strikingly similar.

First, both rely on independent individual work for idea generation. In the Delphi process, isolated and typically anonymous respondents independently write their ideas or reactions to a questionnaire. NGT group members write their ideas on a sheet of paper in silence, in the presence of other group members seated around a table.

Second, individual judgments are pooled in both techniques. Delphi respondents mail their completed questionnaires to the design and monitoring team who, in turn, pool and collate the judgments of the respondent group in a feedback report. In NGT, the judgments of group members are pooled via the round-robin procedure, wherein the ideas of each member are presented to the group and written on a blackboard or flip chart.

Third, both allow for an idea-evaluation stage. In the Delphi process, the monitoring team mails the feedback report to the respondent group, and each respondent independently reads, evaluates, and interprets the ideas on the feedback report. In NGT, the group discusses, verbally clarifies, and evaluates each of the individual ideas of group members that were written on the blackboard or flip chart.

Finally, in both processes, mathematical voting procedures are used (e.g., rank-order or rating methods), and the group decision is arrived at by a mathematical decision rule for aggregating the individual judgments (Huber and Delbecq, 1972).

As indicated above, the major differences between the two processes appear to be:

1) Delphi respondents are typically anonymous to one another, while NGT group members become acquainted with one another.

2) NGT groups meet face to face around a table, while Delphi respondents are physically distant and never meet face to face.

3) All communications between respondents in the Delphi process occur via written questionnaires and feedback reports from the monitoring team. In NGT groups, communications occur directly between members.

INTERACTING, NGT, AND DELPHI PROCESSES

The Delphi Technique was the product of studies of technological forecasting and transfer. The NGT technique was a synthesis of social-psychological group studies. As a result, relatively few researchers have crossed the two traditions to experimentally compare the Delphi Technique with nominal or interacting group methods; however, there are a few notable exceptions.

Gustafson and his associates (1973) tested the comparative effectiveness of independent individuals and interacting, NGT, and Delphi processes on a problem of subjective probability estimation (e.g., "What is the probability that it will rain tomorrow?"). It was found that NGT groups were superior to all other processes in terms of lowest percentage of error and variability of estimations. The Delphi process obtained the poorest outcome, while interacting groups and individuals working independently in nominal groups emerged second and third best, respectively.

Contrary to the findings of Gustafson et al., experiments carried out by Dalkey at Rand (1968, 1969) and Campbell at the University of California (1966) found the Delphi process more effective than interacting meetings. In these experiments, the problem required respondents to estimate the accuracy of a set of facts. The pooled estimates resulting from the Delphi Technique were found more accurate than the estimates resulting from the interacting meetings.

Further comparison

While the above research studies compared decision-making techniques for purposes of probability-estimation problems, one may question whether the research results would be the same if a more real-life, controversial, and emotionally involving problem were chosen. Van de Ven (1974) subjected the NGT, interacting, and Delphi techniques to a formal experimental comparison on an applied problem that was considered by participants to (1) be very difficult; (2) have no solution that would be equally acceptable to all interest groups involved; and (3) evoke highly emotional and subjective responses. Sixty heterogeneous groups (twenty NGT, twenty Delphi, and twenty interacting), each with seven members, were asked to define the job description of a university dormitory counselor. Comparisons between the NGT, Delphi, and interacting groups were based on the quantity of ideas generated and the immediate perceived satisfaction of participants with the decision-making technique in which they had participated. Van de Ven (1974) found that the NGT and Delphi processes generated almost twice as many ideas as interacting groups, and that NGT groups generated slightly more ideas than Delphi groups. In terms of satisfaction, NGT group participants expressed a significantly higher level of satisfaction than did participants in the interacting and Delphi processes. Further, no significant differences were found in perceived group satisfaction between interacting and Delphi techniques.

CHARACTERISTICS
OF GROUP PROCESSES

The above research studies clearly show that on problems requiring groups to generate information, differences exist among NGT, interacting, and Delphi processes. These quantitative findings, however, do not qualitatively explain why such differences exist. A number of researchers have investigated these differences. They found several key process characteristics which are structured into the NGT, Delphi, and interacting techniques which either facilitate or inhibit group performance. These key process characteristics are:

1) *Overall methodology*—the overall structure of decision-making processes.

2) *Role orientation of groups*—the tendency for groups to direct attention toward social roles (e.g., friendship acts or congeniality) or task-oriented roles (e.g., idea giving or judgment sharing).

3) *Search behavior*—the style used by a group to generate task-relevant information, and the amount of effort directed by a group to identify problems.

4) *Normative behavior*—the felt freedom to express ideas in discussions, and the level of conforming behavior in a process.

5) *Equality of participation*—the number of individuals in the group who contribute to search, evaluation, and choice of a group's product or output.

6) *Group composition and size*—the homogeneity or heterogeneity of personnel in a group, as well as the number of individuals involved in the decision-making process.

7) *Method of conflict resolution*—the procedure used by groups to resolve disagreements and conflicts.

8) *Closure to decision process*—the extent to which the meeting arrives at a clear termination point providing an agreed-upon decision and a sense of accomplishment.

9) *Utilization of resources*—the time, cost, and effort involved for administrators and participants in each process.

In the following sections, we will comparatively analyze NGT, Delphi, and interacting processes on these key dimensions.

Role orientations of groups

When an individual works alone, as in the Delphi process, he can focus his entire attention on the problem-solving task. When he works in the presence of others, as in the interacting and NGT processes, then he must also attend to the social, interpersonal obstacles which are dictated by the need for joint task efforts and which are inevitably present when groups meet face to face. For the group member, then, a meeting implies two sets of problems: (1) those which stem directly from the task of problem solving (task-instrumental problems); and (2) those which stem directly from the need to build interpersonal relations with other group members in order to attain the greater problem-solving potential available in the face-to-face group (social-emotional problems). Further, many of the problems created by the presence of other people have no relationship to the task (Collins and Guetzkow, 1964). The greater the amount of effort a decision-making process demands of a group in maintaining social-emotional relationships, the less proportionate time and effort remain for task-instrumental problem solving (Campbell, 1968). It is appropriate, therefore, to compare NGT, Delphi, and interacting processes in terms of task-instrumental versus social-emotional role orientations.

Van de Ven (1974) utilized follow-up questionnaires and interviews with group participants and leaders in order to qualitatively interpret his research results (reported above), and to investigate more deeply the basic characteristics of NGT, Delphi, and interacting groups to account for their clear differences in performance. He reported that the interacting group participants indicated that they most enjoyed the cohesion, friendliness, and agreement among group members, while a majority expressed dislike for the lack of task accomplishment. The interacting group leaders indicated that their groups avoided controversies and heated discussions. Rather, discussions centered around those issues on which group members agreed. Group cohesion and interpersonal relationships, therefore, were developed and maintained around areas of agreement. Clearly, the results that emerged in the interacting groups indicate a predominant orientation toward stimulating and maintaining social-emotional cohesion among members. The participants who aspired to solve the problem, however, felt the process frustrating because of "dangling conversations."

An opposite situation was found in the Delphi groups. Since group members do not meet face to face in the Delphi Technique, there is a complete absence of social-emotional behavior, and all attention focuses on task-instrumental activities. Van de Ven (1974) found, however, that the total absence of interpersonal relationships inhibits task performance because of the lack of verbal clarification or comment on ideas in the feedback report. As anonymous senders and recipients of information, Delphi respondents stated that they did not know to whom they were expressing their ideas or who their group was. Thus, they were unsure of how to express their responses in language understandable to their group. They also questioned whether their interpretations of the ideas in the feedback report were accurate. As a result, 25 percent of the Delphi groups suggested that a discussion with others would be a more interesting and stimulating way to investigate the problem.

NGT stimulates a balanced orientation among group members between task-instrumental and social-emotional concerns. The silent (nominal) period of independent thought and writing forces participants to think and work through the problem. The round-robin listing of ideas followed by a group discussion period clarifies the meaning of each participant's ideas and generates alternative interpretations of the ideas by group members. In the follow-up interviews, a majority of the NGT group leaders reported that while group members appeared to enjoy interaction during the discussion period, with intermittent intervals of laughter and humor, the group remained focused on the task.

Van de Ven (1974) concludes that neither the socially oriented nature of the interacting process, nor the task-oriented nature of the Delphi Technique, are very acceptable to participants or particularly conducive to problem solving. Rather, NGT, which provides a balanced concern for task accomplishment and interpersonal social maintenance functions, appears most acceptable to participants and facilitates problem solving. These qualitative conclusions were quantitatively supported. Van de Ven found no statistical difference between the interacting and Delphi groups concerning perceived group satisfaction, while participants' satisfaction with the NGT process was significantly greater than with either the Delphi or interacting process.

Search behavior

One of the critical process characteristics facilitating creativity is the separation of problems from solutions. Group problem-solving processes which separate ideation (problem identification) from evaluation (solution getting) are superior to group processes which combine them (Brilhart and Jochem, 1964; Maier, 1958; Maier and Hoffman, 1960; Maier and Maier, 1957). According to Maier and Hoffman (1960), "It appears to be a human tendency to seek solutions even before the problem is understood. This tendency to be 'solution-minded' seems to become stronger when there is anxiety over the nature of the decision." Research indicates that the success of problem-solving groups in arriving at creative decisions is related to the proportion of time spent working on the problem (Rotter and Portugal, 1969). Significantly better ideas are generated in the final third period of an individual's independent thought on a topic than in the first two-thirds of the period (Parnes, 1961; Zagona, Ellis, and MacKinnon, 1966). Thus, the quality of group performance can be increased by group processes which (1) retard speedy decisions; and (2) cause the group to perceive the task with an attitude of problem-mindedness as opposed to solution-minded-ness (Maier, 1958; Maier and Solem, 1952).

Van de Ven (1974) found clear differences in the nature of search behavior in NGT, Delphi, and interacting groups. A *reactive search* process, wherein group members tended to react to the opinions of others rather than generate their own ideas, existed in interacting groups. The reactive search process was characterized by short periods of focus on the problem, frequent interruptions and drifting comments by various participants, tangential discussions, and high efforts at maintaining social relationships. Due to the lack of opportunity for group members to independently think through the problem, ideas were expressed as generalizations, and members were reluctant to become specific in their remarks. This was the case even after leaders repeatedly asked members to specifically state what they meant (Van de Ven, 1974). Other researchers have also observed a focus effect in unstructured group meetings, whereby members fall into a rut and pursue a single train of thought for extended periods of discussion (Taylor et al., 1958).

Van de Ven (1974) found that a *proactive search* process existed in the NGT and Delphi processes because each participant was required to write and/or articulate his ideas without the opportunity for other group members to react or evaluate until all ideas were presented. In the Delphi Technique, the respondent group stated that the act of writing responses forced them to think through the problem, and that the repetitive feedback and multiquestionnaire approach was a sensible way to systematically break down a complex problem into workable steps. In addition, written expression of ideas induces a greater feeling of task commitment and a greater sense of permanence than does spoken expression (Bouchard, 1969; Horowitz and Newman, 1964).

Thus, the proactive search behavior that is structured into NGT and the Delphi Technique facilitates problem-mindedness by extending the period of problem-centered focus and by requiring individuals to record their thoughts (Dunnette, 1964; Maier and Solem, 1952; Van de Ven, 1974). The reactive search behavior characteristic of interacting groups results in short, interrupted periods of problem concentration and a tendency to reach speedy decisions before critical dimensions of the problem have been considered (Maier and Hoffman, 1960).

Finally, since NGT and the Delphi Technique structure procedures for decision making, Van de Ven (1974) found high consistency in group performance and low variability in member and leader behavior across groups. However, when interacting meetings are unstructured, high variability in member and leader behavior and in group performance occurs.

Normative behavior

A number of researchers have examined the impact of group norms on the behavior of individuals within a group. In general, research suggests that the normative pressures for conformity prevalent in conventional discussion groups (1) constrain the felt freedom and openness of members to express their ideas; and (2) inhibit creative decision making.

Tersely summarized, the prevalence of conforming behavior in interacting groups seems to relate to the following causes:

> 1) The fact that covert judgments are made by group members even though they are not expressed as overt criticisms in the meeting (Collaros and Anderson, 1969).
>
> 2) The inevitable presence of status incongruities in most organizational groups, wherein low-status participants may be inhibited and go along with opinions expressed by high-status participants (Torrance, 1957).
>
> 3) The implied threat of sanctions from the more knowledgeable members (Hoffman, 1965).
>
> 4) The influence of dominant personality types upon the group (Chung and Ferris, 1971).

NGT minimizes many of the conforming influences of face-to-face group meetings which act to reduce their performance (Van de Ven and Delbecq, 1971). This is due to a number of nonconformance characteristics that are structured into NGT. Because of the nominal phase (silent generation of ideas in writing), the round-robin presenting and recording of ideas on a flip chart, the serial review and clarification of all ideas on the flip chart, and the independent mathematical voting on idea priorities:

> 1) Hidden agendas and covert group dynamics are minimized (Fouriezos, Hatt, and Guetzkow, 1950).
>
> 2) Minority opinions and ideas are more likely to be gen-

erated and voiced (Maier and Hoffman, 1960; Shaw, 1954).

3) Conflicting and incompatible ideas are tolerated in writing (Deutsch, 1949; Guetzkow and Gyr, 1954; Torrance, 1957).

4) All participants are equally expected and given an opportunity to produce their share of ideas and to contribute to the group product (Bales, 1953; Benne and Sheets, 1948).

5) All participants are allowed the opportunity for influencing the direction of group decision outcome (Goldman, Bolen, and Martin, 1961; Maier, 1958; Pelz, 1956).

In a similar manner, the Delphi process minimizes conforming influences because face-to-face discussion is eliminated and respondents are anonymous to one another (Dalkey and Helmer, 1963).

Researchers also suggest that individuals in a group hesitate to identify personal problems when dealing with tasks having social-emotional dimensions (Delbecq and Van de Ven, 1971). They tend to focus upon organizational, institutional, or conventionally accepted problem characteristics. When the social-emotional dimensions of a problem are important and need to be identified, a structured nominal process of separating personal (inside) from institutional or organizational (outside) categories is helpful. For example, in a group setting, elderly persons who were exploring services easily mentioned outside or organizational problems, such as cost of drugs, transportation, etc. Only when they were asked to separately list personal problems did elderly groups bring out areas such as fear of death, loneliness, preoccupation with sickness, feeling disliked by younger people, and other critical social-emotional issues.

Equality of participation

Closely related to normative behavior is the equality of participation among members when contributing to the search, evaluation, and group decision. To the extent that decision making is dominated by a few high-status, expressive, or strong individuals, there will be a lower felt freedom for open discussion and a reduction in the quality of decision making (Chung and Ferris, 1971).

When comparing the evaluations of NGT, interacting, and Delphi participants, Van de Ven (1974) found that only in the interacting process did groups indicate that not all participants felt free to participate and contribute their ideas. There was also a tendency for discussions to polarize on issues and be dominated by a few members, and for issues to be personalized with individuals.

In the NGT groups, on the other hand, there was an absence of felt pressure from dominant individuals, and an expressed freedom to ask objective questions on controversial ideas. Van de Ven (1974) reports that while dominant individuals were the most expressive during the discussion period, they did not take over the meeting because all group members had already had an opportunity to express their views. As a result, the opinions of dominant individuals were simply included in the sample of ideas already under consideration.

Because there is no face-to-face contact among respondents in the Delphi process, there is no opportunity for a few strong individuals to dominate the group's output.

Group size and composition

Numerous researchers have studied group size in terms of number of ideas generated, difficulty in reaching consensus, and patterns of interaction. They have found that, for groups involving interaction, as size increases above some limit (about size seven), restraints against participation also increase and the most active participants become increasingly differentiated. As the size of the group increases, the superiority of NGT over the conventional interacting group increases in terms of the total number of nonoverlapping ideas produced (Carter, Merrowitz, and Lanzetta, 1951; Delbecq, 1968; Gibb, 1951; Hare, 1952; Holloman and Hendrich, 1971; Leader, 1963; South, 1924).

NGT can accommodate larger numbers of participants (up to a limit of approximately nine members) without the dysfunctions of conventional interacting groups (Bouchard and Hare, 1970). There is no limit to the number of participants in a Delphi survey, and the Delphi process is frequently used as a technique to survey one or more target groups. The number of participants is generally determined by the number of respondents required to constitute a representative pooling of judgments for each target group and by the information-processing capability of the design and monitoring team.

Several studies have tested the effects of homogeneous or heterogeneous group composition on problem-solving effectiveness. Heterogeneous groups, characterized by members with widely varying personalities and substantially different perspectives on a problem, were found to produce a higher proportion of high-quality, high-acceptance solutions than homogeneous groups (Hoffman, 1959; Hoffman and Maier, 1961; Hoffman and Smith, 1960). On the other hand, homogeneous groups were found to facilitate group performance because of the reduced likelihood of interpersonal conflict and dominance of the group by one or a few (Grace, 1954; Haythorn, 1953). The mixed results found in these studies suggest that there is value in using the heterogeneous group if its detrimental effects can be controlled. Given the composition of group membership, Bouchard (1969) suggests structured group processes (such as NGT) can facilitate problem solving by (1) specifying clearly the role requirements, i.e., expectations of how participants should behave (Speisman and Moos, 1962); and (2) structuring communication networks, i.e., clarifying when sequential vs. random discussion is desired (Leavitt, 1951).

Method of conflict resolution

N. R. F. Maier (1964) and A. C. Filley (1973, 1974) suggest that disagreement among group members can lead either to hard feelings or to creative decision making, depending upon how it is controlled. Conflict can lead to hard feelings by allowing disagreements to be resolved in personalized emotional pitches, or to be smoothed over by humor or withdrawal. Conflict can lead to creative problem solving by separating persons from problems and attacking the problem rather than the person. In addition, Burke (1970) examined the effect of alternative conflict resolution methods on (1) the constructive use of disagreements; and (2) the perceived satisfaction of conflicting parties with a resolution to disagreements. It was found that withdrawing (remaining silent) and forcing (using status or aggression to dominate) methods as a means to resolve conflict were negatively related to (1) and (2) above. The smoothing-over method was inconsistently related (sometimes positive, sometimes negative). Only confrontation or problem solving always related positively to the above.

Van de Ven (1974) observed that different methods for conflict resolution were generally used in the interacting and NGT groups. In the interacting groups, cohesion and interpersonal relationships developed around areas of agreement. In efforts to maintain these social interrelationships, the interacting groups avoided or smoothed over disagreements by dwelling upon noncontroversial issues. When disagreements did openly emerge, the contending members became polarized on issues, and remarks were personalized during the discussion.

In direct contrast to the problem-solving methods followed to resolve conflicts in the interacting process, the NGT groups confronted disagreements openly and more frequently and depersonalized the problem. Since participants' ideas were recorded on a chart during the round-robin phase of the NGT meeting, during the discussion phase group participants attacked items on the chart—not individuals. Rhetorical, ideological, and emotional comments were more easily transformed into objective problem issues. As a result, groups reported that a positive, constructive attitude toward problem solving emerged among participants in the NGT meetings (Van de Ven, 1974).

Closure to decision process

When comparing the three decision-making processes, Van de Ven (1974) found in his research that in the interacting groups there was less perceived closure, lower felt accomplishment, and lower interest in future phases of problem solving than was true of either NGT or Delphi groups. (NGT and the Delphi Technique, of course, are so structured that they do have a clear termination point.) Van de Ven concluded:

> "The negative reactions of interacting group participants to the task also manifested itself in the severe difficulties leaders encountered in conducting their meetings. Interacting leaders reported a reluctance of groups to get into the task at hand at the beginning of the meeting. Leaders felt much time was wasted in reacting to diversionary questions, personal statements, and ideologies regarding the task. Leaders also indicated they encountered difficulties in concluding their meetings, getting groups to set priorities on the ideas expressed during the meetings, and in arriving at a sense of closure to the meeting" (p. 136).

In direct contrast to the difficulties encountered by interacting leaders, a majority of the NGT leaders reported their groups became sincerely concerned with and motivated by the task at hand, and expressed interest in future phases of the study (Van de Ven, 1974). In terms of closure and felt accomplishment, Delphi groups would score intermediately between interacting and NGT groups.

Utilization of resources

Thus far, attention has been directed toward making quantitative and qualitative comparisons among NGT, interacting, and Delphi processes without regard to the administration of these three procedures. From a practical standpoint, however, the choice of a decision-making procedure in the applied field must also consider the length of time and the amount of administrative cost and effort required to obtain information. This is particularly true when a practitioner needs input from a large number of groups. Suppose, for example, the practitioner is faced with a planning or problem-solving situation which requires information input from multiple reference groups (e.g., consumers, providers, suppliers, administrators, resource controllers, etc.). He or she is offered three alternative processes for obtaining this information: NGT, Delphi, or interacting group techniques. Purely from an administrative perspective of time, cost, and effort, which process should be chosen?

Table 2–1 summarizes the time, cost, and effort for administrators and participants in the 20 NGT, 20 interacting, and 20 Delphi groups conducted in the Van de Ven study. In that study, on the average, the *total administrative working hours* required to prepare for, conduct, and follow through *for one group* was 4.4 hours, 4.2 hours, and 7.1 hours, respectively, for NGT, interacting, and Delphi processes. The *average cost per group* was $11.50 for NGT, $11.00 for interacting, and $22.00 for the Delphi process. The Delphi process required almost twice as much administrative time and cost as did the NGT and interacting groups involving a comparable number of participants.

As indicated in Table 2–1, however, from the participants' perspective the *average working hours per participant* in the Delphi Technique were far less (one-half hour) than in the NGT groups (one and one-half working hours), or in the interacting groups (one and one-quarter working hours). The Delphi process also saved participants the additional time and cost of having to attend face-to-face meetings.

In terms of the *calendar time* required to collect the same information, *on the average,* the NGT or interacting group meetings required four evenings, while a two-round Delphi required five months. Thus, it is clear that the Delphi process requires significantly more calendar time than the other two processes in collecting the same information.

On the basis of time and cost required for *participants,* the

TABLE 2–1. Time, Cost, and Effort in Conducting 20 NGT Groups, 20 Interacting Groups, and 20 Delphi Groups with a Two-Iteration Delphi Survey. Source: Adapted from *Group Decision-Making Effectiveness* by Andrew Van de Ven, published by Center for Business and Economic Research Press, Kent State University, 1974. Used by permission.

Administrative Time and Effort:	NGT	Interacting	Delphi
Physical Preparation Time	20 hrs.	20 hrs.	20 hrs.
Administrative Time in Training Leaders	8 hrs.	4 hrs.	
Time Requirements for 20 Leaders in Conducting Meetings @ 1½ Hours	30 hrs.	30 hrs.	
Post-Meeting Summary Reports	30 hrs.	30 hrs.	
Administrative Time in Follow-up Reminders for Questionnaire #1			29¾ hrs.
Preparation and Distribution of Feedback Reports and Questionnaire #2			30 hrs.
Administrative Time in Follow-up Reminders for Questionnaire #2			41½ hrs.
Administrative Time in Preparing Post-Delphi Summary Reports			20 hrs.
Total Administrative Working Hours	88 hrs.	84 hrs.	141¼ hrs.
Administrative Cost:			
Total Administrative Salary (2.50/hr.)	$220	$210	$353.12
Total Cost of Supplies and Misc.	10	10	86.80
Total Administrative Cost	$230	$220	$439.92
Calendar Time to Conduct Meetings/Delphi	4 evenings	4 evenings	5 months
Participant Time:			
Actual Number of Participants in All Groups	130	138	120
Average Time Requirement per Participant	1½ hr.	1¼ hr.	½ hr.
Total Participant Working Hours	162.5 hrs.	160 hrs.	60 hrs.

Delphi Technique is superior to NGT and interacting groups. If, on the other hand, participants have the time and no large travel costs are entailed in bringing people together, NGT and interacting processes require less *administrative* cost and effort, and the information can be collected in far less calendar time.

SUMMARY PROFILE

Based upon the preceding review of research findings, Table 2–2 presents a recapitulation of the qualitative differences among interacting, NGT, and Delphi groups. The research suggests that different phases of problem solving require different group-process strategies. A profile of the comparative merits of the three decision-making techniques for generating information and group ideas on a problem or issue can now be summarized.

Interacting groups

For *fact-finding problems*, interacting groups contain a number of process characteristics which inhibit decision-making performance:

1) Because interacting group meetings are unstructured, high variability in member and leader behavior occurs from group to group.

2) Discussion tends to fall into a rut, with group members focusing on a single train of thought for extended periods, and with relatively few ideas generated.

3) The absence of an opportunity to think through independent ideas results in a tendency for ideas to be expressed as generalizations.

4) Search behavior is reactive and characterized by short periods of focus on the problem, tendencies for task avoidance, tangential discussions, and high efforts in establishing social relationships and generating social knowledge.

5) High-status, expressive, or strong personality-type individuals tend to dominate in search, evaluation, and choice of group product.

6) Meetings tend to conclude with a high perceived lack

TABLE 2–2.   Comparison of Qualitative Differences Among Interacting, NGT, and Delphi Groups.
Source: Adapted from *Group Decision-Making Effectiveness* by Andrew Van de Ven, published by Center for Business and Economic Research Press, Kent State University, 1974. Used by permission.

DIMENSION	INTERACTING	NGT	DELPHI
OVERALL METHODOLOGY	Unstructured meeting High variability between decision-making groups	Structured meeting Low variability between decision-making groups	Structured series of questionnaires and feedback reports Low variability between decision panels
ROLE ORIENTATION OF GROUPS	Social-emotional focus	Balanced social-emotional and task-instrumental focus	Task-instrumental focus
RELATIVE QUANTITY OF IDEAS	Low; focused "rut" effect	High; independent thinking	High; isolated thinking
RELATIVE QUALITY AND SPECIFICITY OF IDEAS	Low quality Generalizations	High quality High specificity	High quality High specificity
NORMATIVE BEHAVIOR	Inherent conformity pressures	Tolerance for nonconformity	Freedom not to conform
SEARCH BEHAVIOR	Reactive Short problem focus Task avoidance tendency New social knowledge	Proactive Extended problem focus High task-centeredness New social and task knowledge	Proactive Controlled problem focus High task-centeredness New task knowledge
EQUALITY OF PARTICIPATION	Member dominance	Member equality	Respondent equality in pooling of independent judgments
METHODS OF CONFLICT RESOLUTION	Person-centered Smoothing over and withdrawal	Problem-centered Confrontation and problem solving	Problem-centered Majority rule of pooled independent judgments
CLOSURE TO DECISION PROCESS	Lack of closure Low felt accomplishment	High closure High felt accomplishment	High closure Medium felt accomplishment
TASK MOTIVATION	Medium	High	Medium

of closure, low felt accomplishment, and low interest in future phases of problem solving.

There are, however, a number of techniques that can be adopted during conventional discussion group meetings to improve their performance. When there is a need to obtain the ideas of all group members on a problem or issue to be discussed, the round-robin technique can be very helpful. This technique facilitates the self-disclosure of ideas even by less secure members who may hesitate to bring some problem dimensions before the group in the conventional interacting situation (Culbert, 1968). Further, the round-robin procedure of writing problem dimensions and issues on a blackboard or flip chart reduces arguments over semantics, increases retention of ideas presented, and decreases redundancy of discussions (Delbecq and Van de Ven, 1971). Finally, evaluation and synthesis of issues can be improved in discussion groups by having the total set of ideas or issues placed in writing before the group prior to spontaneous discussion of each idea.

It should be noted, however, that interacting groups can play a very positive role with respect to: (1) increasing group motivation and cohesion; (2) increasing a sense of group consensus; and (3) increasing the feeling that each alternative solution possibility has been carefully reviewed. Thus, for certain motivational purposes, the problems associated with the interacting group may not cancel out its benefits.

NGT

NGT is a structured group meeting which follows a prescribed sequence of problem-solving steps. The NGT process includes a number of characteristics which facilitate decision-making performance:

1) Low variability among groups in member and leader behavior leads to consistency in decision making.

2) A balanced concern for social-emotional group maintenance roles and performance of task-instrumental roles offers both social reinforcement and task accomplishment reward to group members.

3) The silent independent generation of ideas, followed by further thought and listening during the round-robin procedure, results in a high quantity of ideas.

4) Search behavior is proactive, characterized by extended

periods in generating and clarifying alternative dimensions of the problem, tendencies for high task-centered group effort, and the generation of new social and task-related knowledge.

5) The structured process forces equality of participation among members in generating information on the problem.

6) NGT meetings tend to conclude with a perceived sense of closure, accomplishment, and interest in future phases of problem solving.

Associated with the positive characteristics of NGT are difficulties that are frequently encountered in conducting NGT meetings. While these difficulties and possible solutions will be discussed in detail in Chapter 3, they include:

1) Extended preparation for NGT meetings is necessary to clearly identify the information desired from a group, and to provide the necessary supplies. NGT, therefore, is not a spontaneous group meeting technique.

2) Inflexibility of the structured NGT format makes it difficult to make adjustments or to change topics in the middle of a meeting. NGT is generally limited, therefore, to a single-purpose, single-topic meeting.

3) Conforming behavior to a structured format is required on the part of all participants, a condition which is not immediately comfortable to inexperienced participants.

The Delphi Technique

The Delphi process is a survey technique for decision making among isolated anonymous respondents. The characteristics of the Delphi process which facilitate decision-making performance are:

1) The isolated generation of ideas in writing produces a high quantity of ideas.

2) The process of writing responses to the questions forces respondents to think through the complexity of the problem, and to submit specific, high-quality ideas.

3) Search behavior is proactive since respondents cannot react to the ideas of others.

4) The anonymity and isolation of respondents provides freedom from conformity pressures.

5) Simple pooling of independent ideas and judgments facilitates equality of participants.

6) The Delphi process tends to conclude with a moderate perceived sense of closure and accomplishment.

7) The technique is valuable for obtaining judgments from experts geographically isolated.

The major characteristics of the Delphi process which inhibit decision-making performance are:

1) The lack of opportunity for social-emotional rewards in problem solving leads to a feeling of detachment from the problem-solving effort.

2) The lack of opportunity for verbal clarification or comment on the feedback report creates communication and interpretation difficulties among respondents.

3) Conflicting or incompatible ideas on the feedback report are handled by simply pooling and adding the votes of group respondents. Thus, while this majority rule procedure identifies group priorities, conflicts are not resolved.

This chapter has summarized research on NGT, Delphi, and interacting groups concerned with judgmental problem solving. The present burden of evidence favors NGT and Delphi approaches to idea or estimate generation, interaction for purposes of clarification, and mathematical voting in the form of rank-ordering or rating for aggregating group judgments. Chapters 3 and 4 will detail NGT and Delphi formats which combine these group processes at different stages of analysis. Both techniques should greatly enhance the quality of group effort for judgmental tasks.

REFERENCES

Bales, R. F. "The Equilibrium Problem in Small Groups." In *Working Papers in the Theory of Action*. T. Parsons, R. F. Bales, and E. A. Shils. Free Press, 1953.

Benne, K. A., and P. Sheets. "Functional Roles of Group Numbers."
    Journal of Social Issues, 2 (1948): 42–47.
Bouchard, T. J., Jr. "Personality, Problem-Solving Procedure, and Per-
    formance in Small Groups." *Journal of Applied Psychology*,
    53, 1, Part 2 (February 1969): 1–29.
Bouchard, T. J., Jr., and M. Hare. "Size, Performance, and Potential in
    Brainstorming Groups." *Journal of Applied Psychology*, 54, 1
    (February 1970): 51–55.
Brilhart, J. K., and L. M. Jochem. "The Effects of Different Patterns
    on Outcomes of Problem-Solving Discussions." *Journal of
    Applied Psychology*, 48 (1964): 175–79.
Burke, R. J. "Methods of Resolving Superior-Subordinate Conflict:
    The Constructive Use of Subordinate Differences and Dis-
    agreements." *Organization Behavior and Human Performance*,
    5 (1970): 393–411.
Campbell, J. P. "Individual versus Group Problem Solving in an
    Industrial Sample." *Journal of Applied Psychology*, 52, 3
    (1968): 205–10.
Campbell, R. M. "A Methodological Study of the Utilization of Experts
    in Business Forecasting." Doctoral dissertation, University of
    California, Los Angeles, 1966.
Carter, L. F., A. Haythorn, B. Merrowitz, and J. Lanzetta. "The Rela-
    tion of Categorizations and Ratings in the Observation of
    Group Behavior." *Human Relations*, 4 (1951).
Chung, K. H., and M. J. Ferris. "An Inquiry of the Nominal Group
    Process." *Academy of Management Journal*, 14, 4 (1971): 520–
    24.
Collaros, P. A., and L. R. Anderson. "The Effect of Perceived Expert-
    ness upon Creativity of Members of Brainstorming Groups."
    Journal of Applied Psychology, 53, 2 (April 1969): 159–63.
Collins, B., and H. Guetzkow. *A Social Psychology of Group Processes
    for Decision Making*. Wiley, 1964.
Culbert, S. A. "Trainer Self-Disclosure and Member Growth in Two
    T-Groups." *Journal of Applied Behavioral Sciences*, 4, 1,
    (1968): 47–74.
Dalkey, N. C. *Experiment in Group Prediction*. Rand Corporation,
    1968.
Dalkey, N. C. *The Delphi Method: An Experimental Study of Group
    Opinion*. Rand Corporation, June 1969.
Dalkey, N. C., and O. Helmer. "An Experimental Application of the
    Delphi Method to the Use of Experts." *Management Science*
    (1963).

Delbecq, A. L. "The World Within the 'Span of Control': Managerial Behavior in Groups of Varied Size." *Business Horizons* (August 1968).

Delbecq, A. L., and A. H. Van de Ven. "A Group Process Model for Problem Identification and Program Planning." *Journal of Applied Behavioral Sciences*, 7, 4 (July–August 1971).

Deutsch, M. "An Experimental Study of the Effects of Cooperation and Competition on Group Process." *Human Relations*, 2 (1949): 199–231.

Dunnette, M. "Are Meetings Any Good for Problem Solving?" *Personnel Administration* (March–April 1964): 12–29.

Dunnette, M., J. Campbell, and K. Jaastad. "The Effect of Group Participation on Brainstorming Effectiveness for Two Industrial Samples." *Journal of Applied Psychology*, 47, 1 (1963): 30–37.

Filley, A. C. *Organization Invention: A Study of Utopian Organizations.* Bureau of Business Research and Service, University of Wisconsin, Madison, Graduate School of Business, 1973.

Filley, A. C. *Interpersonal Conflict Resolution.* Scott, Foresman and Company, 1974.

Fouiezos, N. T., M. L. Hatt, and H. Guetzkow. "Measurement of Self-Oriented Needs in Discussion Groups." *Journal of Abnormal and Social Psychology*, 45 (1950): 682–90.

Gibb, J. R. "The Effects of Size and of Threat Reduction upon Creativity in Problem-Solving Situations." *American Psychologist*, 6 (1951).

Goldman, M., M. Bolen, and R. Martin. "Some Conditions Under Which Groups Operate and How This Affects Their Performance." *Journal of Social Psychology*, 54 (1961): 47–56.

Grace, H. A. "Conformance and Performance." *Journal of Social Psychology*, 40 (1954): 333–35.

Guetzkow, H., and J. Gyr. "An Analysis of Conflict in Decision-Making Groups." *Human Relations*, 7 (1954): 367–82.

Gustafson, D. H., R. M. Shukla, A. L. Delbecq, and G. W. Walster. "A Comparative Study of Differences in Subjective Likelihood Estimates Made by Individuals, Interacting Groups, Delphi Groups, and Nominal Groups." *Organizational Behavior and Human Performance*, 9 (1973): 280–91.

Hall, E. J., J. Mouton, and R. R. Blake. "Group Problem-Solving Effectiveness Under Conditions of Pooling versus Interaction." *Journal of Social Psychology*, 59 (1963): 147–57.

Hare, A. P. "A Study of Interaction and Consensus in Different-Sized Groups." *American Sociological Review*, 17 (1952): 261–67.

Haythorn, A. "The Influence of Individual Members on the Characteristics of Small Groups." *Journal of Abnormal and Social Psychology,* 48 (1953): 276–84.

Hoffman, L. R. "Homogeneity of Member Personality and Its Effect on Group Problem Solving." *Journal of Abnormal and Social Psychology,* 58 (1959): 27–32.

Hoffman, L. R. "Group Problem Solving." In *Advances in Experimental Social Psychology,* Part II. L. Berkowitz, ed. Academic Press, 1965.

Hoffman, L. R., and N. R. F. Maier. "Quality and Acceptance of Problem Solutions by Members of Homogeneous and Heterogeneous Groups." *Journal of Abnormal and Social Psychology,* 62 (1961): 401–407.

Hoffman, L. R., and G. G. Smith. "Some Factors Affecting the Behavior of Members of Problem-Solving Groups." *Sociometry,* 23 (1960): 273–91.

Holloman, C. R., and H. W. Hendrich. "Problem Solving in Different-Sized Groups." *Personnel Psychology,* 24 (1971): 489–500.

Horowitz, M. W., and J. B. Newman. "Spoken and Written Expression: An Experimental Analysis." *Journal of Abnormal and Social Psychology,* 68 (1964): 640–47.

Huber, G., and A. L. Delbecq. "Guidelines for Combining the Judgment of Individual Members in Decision Conferences." *Academy of Management Journal,* 15, 2 (June 1972): 161–74.

Leader, A. "Patterns in Judgmental Decision Making: Individual and Group Performance Across Tasks." Unpublished doctoral dissertation, Indiana University Graduate School of Business, 1963.

Leavitt, H. J. "Some Effects of Certain Communication Patterns on Group Performance." *Journal of Abnormal and Social Psychology,* 46 (1951): 38–50.

Maier, N. R. F. *The Appraisal Interview: Objectives, Methods, and Skills.* Wiley, 1958.

Maier, N. R. F., and L. R. Hoffman. "Quality of First and Second Solution in Group Problem Solving." *Journal of Applied Psychology,* 44, 4 (1960): 278–83.

Maier, N. R. F., and A. R. A. Maier. "An Experimental Test of the Effects of 'Developmental' Group Decisions." *Journal of Applied Psychology,* 41 (1957): 320–23.

Maier, N. R. F., and A. R. Solem. "The Contribution of the Discussion Leader to the Quality of Group Thinking." *Human Relations,* 3 (1952): 155–74.

Osborn, A. F. *Applied Imagination*. Scribners, 1957.

Parnes, S. J. "Effects of Extended Effort in Creative Problem Solving." *Journal of Educational Psychology*, 52 (1961): 117–22.

Parnes, S. J., and A. Meadow. "Effects of Brainstorming Instructions on Creative Problem Solving by Trained and Untrained Subjects." *Journal of Educational Psychology*, 50 (1959): 171–76.

Pelz, D. C. "Some Social Factors Related to Performance in a Research Organization." *Administrative Science Quarterly*, 1 (1956): 310–25.

Rotter, G. S., and S. M. Portugal. "Group and Individual Effects in Problem Solving." *Journal of Applied Psychology*, 53, 4 (August 1969): 338–41.

Shaw, M. E. "Some Effects of Problem Solution Efficiency in Different Communication Nets." *Journal of Experimental Psychology*, 48 (1954):211–17.

South, E. B. "Some Psychological Aspects of Committee Work." *Journal of Applied Psychology*, 2 (1924).

Speisman, J. C., and R. H. Moos. "Group Compatibility and Production." *Journal of Abnormal and Social Psychology*, 54 (1962): 190–96.

Taylor, D. W., P. L. Berry, and C. H. Block. "Does Group Participation When Using Brainstorming Facilitate or Inhibit Creative Thinking?" *Administrative Science Quarterly*, 3 (1958): 23–47.

Torrance, E. P. "Group Decision Making and Disagreement." *Social Forces*, 35 (1957): 314–18.

Van de Ven, A. H. *Group Decision-Making Effectiveness*. Kent State University Center for Business and Economic Research Press, 1974.

Van de Ven, A. H., and A. L. Delbecq. "Nominal versus Interacting Group Processes for Committee Decision-Making Effectiveness." *Academy of Management Journal*, 14, 2 (June 1971): 203–12.

Vroom, V. H., L. D. Grant, and T. J. Cotton. "The Consequences of Social Interaction in Group Problem Solving." *Journal of Applied Psychology*, 53, 4 (August 1969): 338–41.

Zogona, S. V., J. E. Ellis, and W. J. MacKinnon. "Group Effectiveness in Creative Problem-Solving Tasks: An Examination of Relevant Variables." *Journal of Psychology*, 62 (1966): 111–37.

Guidelines for Conducting NGT Meetings

3

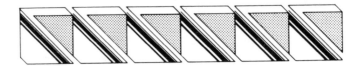

In order to illustrate the NGT process, it will be useful to set up an imaginary meeting situation. We will use the case of twenty participants from various large organizations, attending a training conference on group techniques. Our illustration will be a demonstration NGT meeting, the purpose of which is to allow participants to develop questions concerning how to conduct such meetings in back-home settings.

There is a secondary benefit in selecting this particular case illustration. The illustrated meeting format has been shown to be an effective training device which readers may wish to use as a means to introduce other individuals to NGT.

PREPARATORY TASKS

The leader should see that a number of preliminary steps are taken care of before the actual NGT meeting gets underway. These include: selecting and preparing the meeting room, providing the necessary supplies, and presenting the opening statement.

The meeting room

The major activities of an NGT meeting take place in small groups. The leader must therefore choose a meeting room large enough to accommodate the participants in groups of from five to nine members at individual tables. It is also important that the tables be spaced far enough apart so that the noise and activity at one table does not interfere with other tables.

Although a variety of seating arrangements are serviceable, the focus of an NGT meeting is on the *list* of ideas placed on a flip chart rather than on individual participants. Therefore, it is helpful to seat participants at a rectangular table arranged as an open "U" with a flip chart at the open end of the table (Figure 3–1). Having a serviceable writing area is also helpful, as the meeting begins with a period of independent written activity.

Supplies

The following supplies should be provided at NGT meetings:

1) Flip chart for each table.
2) Roll of masking tape.
3) Pack of 3 × 5 cards for each table.
4) Felt pens for each table.
5) Paper and pencil for each participant.

The use of the various items will become apparent as we proceed with the description of the meeting. At the moment, however, a word about flip charts is worthwhile.

NGT meetings rely heavily on writing ideas in front of each small group. Therefore, a flip chart or some similar device is imperative. Alternatives to flip charts, which are sometimes unavailable, are: sheets of newsprint, poster board, a roll of butcher paper which may be cut into sheets, or large blackboards (since all items need to be retained in front of each group for voting, the small blackboard is generally undesirable).

Welcoming statement

When individuals come together to engage in group tasks, perceptions of why the group was formed will affect performance. For

FIGURE 3–1.   Meeting Room Arrangement for Three NGT Tables.

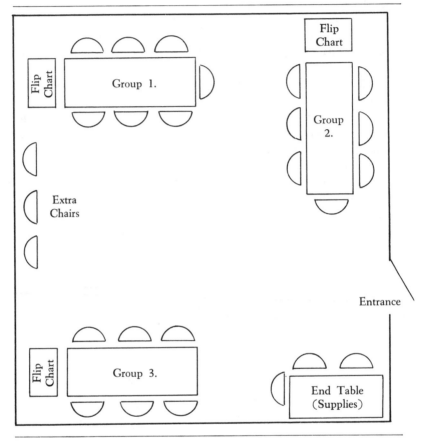

example, members who perceive that their group was formed on the basis of congeniality will proceed in a congenial but less effective problem-solving manner than will group members who perceive they were gathered together because of their analytic abilities and problem-solving skills. It is important, therefore, that the NGT leader clarify the member roles and group objectives for the meeting. Appropriate role definitions will help reduce status barriers among members, encourage free communication, and decrease the tendency for high-status individuals to be unduly verbal.

Thus, the leader's welcoming statement should include:

1) A cordial and warm welcome.

2) A sense of importance concerning the group's task.

3) Clarification of the importance of each member's contribution.

4) An indication of the use or purpose of the meeting's output.

We can exemplify such an introduction by going back to our illustration meeting of twenty participants from large organizations gathered to learn about the NGT technique. The leader of the meeting might begin as follows:

"I want to express my appreciation to each of you for attending this workshop on NGT. I am aware that there are many other training opportunities as well as informal activities going on at our convention at the present time. I appreciate the sacrifice you have made to take advantage of this workshop. I welcome each of you warmly to this session.

"Our objective is an important one. At the conclusion of this meeting, we should be able to anticipate and answer many of the questions and difficulties which administrators face when trying to utilize the NGT process. Obviously, unless we are prepared to meet these challenges, our ability to successfully implement this useful technique will be very limited.

"In our meeting it is important that *each* of us fully participate. Indeed, success will depend on our equal and full participation. Each of us is here as an important group resource. There are no status differences between us in this particular meeting. Our success depends on every member fully sharing the insight from his or her own administrative, professional, or technical perspective. I appreciate, therefore, the willingness of every one of you to fully share your ideas and work intensely during the next ninety minutes we are together.

"The ideas which you generate in this workshop will become the basis for follow-up training, skill development, and discussion."

THE NGT PROCESS

For purposes of illustration, we will now focus on a single table of six or seven group members, with a leader who also serves as a recorder. As we will discuss later in the chapter, it is possible to have

one leader to provide process directions to several tables, in which
case it would be necessary to have a trained recorder at individual
tables.

Step 1: Silent generation
of ideas in writing

The first step in an NGT meeting is to have the group
members write key ideas silently and independently. As indicated in
Chapter 2, the benefits of this step are:

1) Adequate time for thinking and reflection.
2) Social facilitation (that is, the constructive tension
created by observing other group members working hard).
3) Avoidance of interruptions.
4) Avoidance of undue focusing on a particular idea or
train of thought.
5) Sufficient time for search and recall.
6) Avoidance of competition, status pressures, and conformity pressures.
7) The benefit of remaining problem-centered.
8) Avoidance of choosing between ideas prematurely.

In order to facilitate these benefits, the leader proceeds to in-
struct the group in the first step of the process by:

1) Presenting the nominal question to the group in written
form.
2) Verbally reading the question.
3) Directing the group to write ideas in brief phrases or
statements.
4) Asking the group to work silently and independently.
5) Modeling good group behavior.

To proceed with our meeting example, the leader would carry
on as follows:

"Would each of you please look carefully at the question
at the top of the worksheet which I am going to hand out."

The leader passes a set of worksheets to each table. Worksheets are simply lined tablet paper with the nominal question written at the top.

> "You will notice that the question which is the focus of our meeting is the following: What barriers do you anticipate in trying to use the NGT technique back home?
>
> "I would like each of you to take five minutes to list your ideas in response to this question, in a brief phrase or a few words, on the worksheet in front of you. Please work independently of other members in identifying barriers which *you* anticipate in trying to use NGT back home. During this period of independent thinking I ask that you not talk to other members, interrupt their thinking, or look at their worksheets. Since this is the opportunity for each of us to prepare his or her contributions to the meeting, I would appreciate intense effort during the next five minutes. At the end of five minutes, I will call time and suggest how we can proceed to share our ideas. Are there any questions? Let's proceed then with our individual effort for the next five minutes."

The leader turns to his own worksheet and begins to write.

Step 1 guidelines • There are four key guidelines for serving as leader in Step 1:

1) Resist nonprocess clarifications.
2) Have the question in writing.
3) Model good group behavior by writing in silence.
4) Sanction individuals who disrupt the silent independent activity.

Later in this chapter we will talk about writing nominal questions. For the moment, it is important to note that once the question is written and pretested, the leader should avoid providing answers to the question for the group. Experimental evidence clearly shows that a leader who engages in detailed clarification of group tasks tends to lead the group toward his or her interpretation of the task. In this case, the more the leader "clarifies" the question by providing exemplary answers, the more the group focuses on the leader's frame of reference.

For example, if the leader in our case illustration was asked: "By barriers, do you mean lack of necessary skills?" and answered by saying: "Sure, that might be a barrier. For example, perhaps the person trying to use the technique back home did not have prior experience with the technique," he or she will have led the group to focus on leadership skills as a barrier. In fact, for the particular group of administrators present, other barriers such as status impediments, group compositions, etc., might be far more important.

The appropriate answer the leader should give is: "Any barrier which comes to your mind should be written on your worksheet."

If a member of the group still asks for greater clarification of the question, a useful technique is for the leader to answer: "Think of the question as an inkblot. I want you to look at the words on the worksheet and write those ideas which come to *your* mind when you read the question." Such a response is obviously dependent on having the question in writing in front of the group members.

As alternatives to worksheets, the leader can write the stimulus question on a flip chart in front of the group. In any case, having the question in writing clearly aids group concentration on the appropriate question and decreases need for clarification.

The NGT leader is normally not an outsider to the meeting, but rather a working participant. As such, he or she should provide a model of appropriate group behavior during the silent generation phase. A leader who is working hard at the task provides an example of good group behavior. A leader who distracts the group by engaging in other tasks, talking to people, or wandering around the room increases the tendency for other members to deviate from silent, independent reflection and writing.

If individuals in the group begin to whisper to each other, leave their places, sigh, or otherwise disrupt the silent writing period, it is important that the leader quickly and impersonally sanction the distracting behavior. The simplest and most effective method is to look away from the violating parties and speak to the entire group saying, "I hope that we won't interrupt those who are still at work by talking or moving about. There are still two minutes remaining in our work period, and I ask that we continue to think and write our ideas down in silence for the remainder of this short period."

Step 2: Round-robin recording of ideas

The second step of NGT is to record the ideas of group members on a flip chart visible to the entire group. Round-robin recording means going around the table and asking for one idea from one member at a time. The leader writes the idea of a group member on the flip chart and then proceeds to ask for one idea from the next group member in turn. Figure 3–2 presents a typical list of ideas generated by a group in response to the question used in our case illustration. As indicated in Chapter 2, the benefits of round-robin recording are:

1) Equal participation in the presentation of ideas.
2) Increase in problem-mindedness.
3) Depersonalization—the separation of ideas from personalities.
4) Increase in the ability to deal with a larger number of ideas.
5) Tolerance of conflicting ideas.
6) Encouragement of hitchhiking.[1]
7) Provision of a written record and guide.

There is general agreement among scholars that the sharing of all ideas and equalization of participation increases group creativity. The rather mechanical format of going to each member in turn to elicit ideas establishes an important behavior pattern. By the second or third round of idea giving, each member is an achieved participant in the group. A precedent for further participation has been accomplished without competition with high-status members, more aggressive personalities, or more emotional members.

A major concern in group meetings is problem-centeredness. Chapter 2 documented the importance of a group identifying all the elements of a problem and avoiding premature problem definition. By listing the entire array of ideas *before* discussion and voting, the group ensures that significant ideas will not get lost or forgotten. Lists also facilitate hitchhiking and allow for the consideration of conflicting ideas without pressure.

The fact that a list is *written* is of particular importance. A written idea is more objective and less personal than a verbal statement. If the idea is in writing, individuals are better able to separate it from the personality or position of the individual contributing it. Also, groups are able to deal with a larger number of ideas in writing. As a

1. *Hitchhiking as used here refers to the fact that ideas listed on the flip chart by one member may stimulate another member to think of an idea he had not written on his worksheet during the silent period. In this case, he is free to add the new idea to his worksheet and report it for listing on the flip chart when his turn arrives.*

FIGURE 3–2.   List of Items Generated in Response to Question: "What barriers do you anticipate in trying to use the NGT technique back home?"

1. Leader dominance
2. Lack of ability to write a good nominal question
3. Uncertainty about who should be invited
4. Resistance to a structured group process
5. Lack of skill in conducting this type of meeting
6. Length of time the process takes
7. Avoiding redundancy in the listing process
8. Avoiding dominance in discussion of items
9. Unequal writing skill among group members
10. Shyness in exposing one's own items
11. Size of the group may be too large to use technique
12. How to get critical individuals to attend
13. Resistance of high-status people to open discussion
14. Lack sufficient self-confidence to run unfamiliar meeting
15. Inadequate leader legitimacy
16. Inadequate physical facilities
17. Insufficient motivation to work seriously
18. Artificial redundancy in a long list

rough rule of thumb, individuals remember 40 percent of what they can hear, but 70 percent of what they can both see and hear. The written list also becomes the group's secretary, providing minutes and a working draft for later refinement.

Going from member to member eliciting only one idea at a time has its benefits as well. It is not unusual for as much as a third of an individual's ideas relative to a problem to remain unspoken. Embarrassment, conservatism, fear of self-disclosure, etc., contribute much to the often spoken of "hidden agenda." In pilot studies, individual group members were asked to present their entire list to the group at one time. The effects were to: (1) have members hide a substantial number of ideas; and (2) decrease the depersonalization of ideas since it was easy to identify a cluster of ideas with an individual. Round-robin listing minimizes both negative features. First, individuals are given models for self-disclosure. The example of early risk-takers encourages other group members to present more controversial ideas. Second, as the list progresses in length, it is more and more difficult and less rewarding to try to remember who presented what idea. Instead, the list becomes a depersonalized group product.

Finally, the written list is an important early group reward. Members are impressed with the array of ideas generated by the group, the amount of overlap of ideas providing areas of agreement and consensus, the differentiated contributions of individual group members, and the immediate richness of resources for further analysis. At the same time, the group is protected against premature focus on selected ideas or problem simplification.

Inasmuch as round-robin listing is at the heart of the NGT feedback process, careful attention to this step is warranted.

Step 2 guidelines • Leader requirements for this step include:

1) Clear verbal statement of the step:
    a. the objective is to map the group's thinking.
    b. ideas should be presented in brief words or phrases.
    c. ideas will be taken serially.
    d. duplicate items should be omitted.
    e. variations on themes are desirable.
2) Effective mechanical recording.
3) Direct sanction of inappropriate group behavior.

To return to our illustration, the leader would begin Step 2 with the following statement:

"During the last five minutes, each of us has used our worksheets to list important barriers to utilizing the NGT technique back home. Now I would like to have each of you share your ideas with the other members of the group.

"This is an important step because our list of ideas will constitute a guide for further discussion, help us understand the richness of ideas we have to work with, and stimulate additional ideas.

"In order to accomplish this goal as quickly and efficiently as possible, I am going to go around the table and ask individuals, one at a time, to give me one idea from their worksheet, summarized in a brief phrase or a few words. After the entire list is on the board, we will have the opportunity to discuss, clarify, and dispute the ideas.

"If someone else in the group lists an idea which you also had on your worksheet, you need not repeat the idea. If, however, in *your judgment* the idea on your worksheet contains a different emphasis or variation, we would welcome the idea.

Variations on a theme are important and will help us be creative.

[Turning to the first person] "Mr. Smith, would you give me one idea from your list?"

The leader then proceeds to list the ideas on the flip chart, numbering each idea as it is written on the chart. Usually after the second time around the table, one member of the group will say: "I don't have any further ideas." The leader should respond: "Fine, Joe, you can pass. However, feel free to take another turn if some other idea occurs to you." Thus, the individuals who pass will feel free to reenter the listing exercise when their turn comes up on subsequent rounds. The leader should take a turn each round also, listing one idea from his or her worksheet just like the members.

Recording guidelines • Serving as recorder is a natural skill for some individuals, but a skill others must develop. There are several important hints for effective recording:

1) Record ideas as rapidly as possible.

2) Record ideas in the words used by the group member.

3) Provide assistance in abbreviating only in special situations.

4) Make the entire list visible to the group by tearing off completed sheets from the flip chart and taping them to the wall.

A group's patience is short during the listing of ideas. It is important, therefore, for the leader to complete the step as quickly as possible. Rapid writing (not easy for most of us to master consistent with legibility) is a goal to attain.

It is also important to put the ideas up on the flip chart in the words used by the group member. For example, if the member presents an idea as "what are the physical requirements" these are the words that should appear on the chart. Writing "facilities needed" or some other leader's expression is a violation of etiquette, but more important, decreases the member's role and unduly enlarges the leader's role.

There are situations where individuals seem incapable of presenting their ideas in brief statements. A member might say: "The need for adequate physical facilities limits the effectiveness of the technique to special situations and physical locations." Recorders will soon wear out their felt pens and patience dealing with such lengthy statements. It is appropriate to ask members: "Could you think of a slightly shorter way of placing the idea on the flip chart?" The burden of abbreviation can thus be sent back to the member. A stubborn member who seems determined to speak in epistles rather than phrases can be disciplined by saying: "Would you think about that idea for a few minutes and I will come back to you and ask for a few words or short phrase we can place on the chart." Then the leader can continue, and return to the wordy group member after two or three others have given their ideas. In rare situations (usually research situations with individuals of very limited education) it is appropriate for the recorder to help a member summarize or abbreviate ideas. This, however, should be avoided where possible. The advantages of using the words of the group member are: (1) an increased perception of equality and member importance; (2) greater ego identification with the task; and (3) a lack of feeling that the leader-recorder is manipulating the group.

Members of NGT groups will sometimes engage in one of several disruptive behaviors during the round-robin listing phase. These include: trying to discuss ideas rather than list them; arguing with ideas as they are presented; asking the leader to rule on duplications; and engaging in side conversations. All of these behaviors should be sanctioned when they occur. A member who says: "I'm not quite sure of this idea. Perhaps we should talk about it before we put it on the list," should be encouraged to simply list the idea with an indication that adequate discussion time for all ideas will follow.

The decision as to whether an item is the same as or different from an earlier idea should not be debated. Place responsibility back on the group member by saying, "If *you* feel your idea is slightly different, let's put it up on the chart."

The goal of Step 2, then, is a rapid, accurate list of ideas in brief words or phrases, recorded in writing on a flip chart in front of the entire group. This list becomes the guide for further discussion and a depersonalized mapping of the group's ideation.

Step 3: Serial discussion for clarification

The third step of NGT is to discuss each idea in turn.[2] The benefits of this step are:

> 2. In Chapter 2, it was pointed out that interaction has a positive impact on evaluation. The benefit of discussion seems to relate primarily to the opportunity for increased clarification, information giving, and the sharing of analysis and logic behind judgments. This opportunity for clarification accounts for the tendency of group judgment to be superior to isolated individual judgments.

1) Avoidance of focusing unduly on any particular idea or subset of ideas.

2) Opportunity for clarification and elimination of misunderstanding.

3) Opportunity to provide the logic behind arguments and disagreements.

4) Recording of differences of opinion without undue argumentation.

Serial discussion means taking each idea listed on the flip chart in order, and allowing a short period of time for the discussion of each idea. The leader points to Item 1, reads it out loud, and asks the group if there are any questions, statements of clarification, or statements of agreement or disagreement which members would like to make about it. The leader allows for discussion, and then moves the group on to Item 2, Item 3, etc.

The dynamics of the resulting communication concerning each idea are important to understand. First, the central object of the discussion is to clarify, not to win arguments. In its simplest form, clarification helps other members understand the meaning of the brief words or phrases on the chart. (It is hardly necessary to belabor the point that written communication is often subject to misunderstanding.) After a brief explanation of what is meant by a specific set of words, most members will reliably record their judgments about the item even if the phrase or words used on the flip chart are awkward.

Clarification is not restricted, however, to comments concerning what the words expressing an item "mean." In the brief discussion, members of the group can convey the logic or analysis behind the item, and the relative importance they place on the item. Likewise, individuals can express their agreement or disagreement with either the expressed logic or the felt relative importance.

Unfortunately, expressions of disagreement in groups can become the signals for lobbying, aggressive interaction, or disruptive argumentation. Most individuals are intuitively aware that prominence and aggression in interaction are highly associated with influence over meeting outcomes in conventional discussion settings. Thus, in other types of meetings, an aggressive or high-status group member can often dominate the group's formal outcome even though other members still disagree with his or her logic.

The purpose of serial discussion is to enhance clarification but minimize influence based on verbal prominence or status. To accomplish these dual objectives, the leader should "pace" the discussion, i.e., he or she should not allow discussion to: (1) unduly focus on any particular idea; or (2) degenerate into argumentation. Suppose, for example, Member X feels that Item 7 is very important, and Member Y feels that Item 7 is specious. The role of the leader is to allow both points of view to be aired, but then to move the group on to a discussion of Item 8, since the purpose of serial discussion is to disclose thinking and analysis, not to resolve differences of opinion. Differences of opinion will be accurately recorded in the voting procedure.

Likewise, if the group spends most of its time discussing the first six items, and very little time discussing later items, those later items may suffer from lack of adequate clarification. The leader should attempt, therefore, to balance discussion across all items, making sure that no item suffers from inadequate clarification due to time constraints.

Step 3 guidelines • The main responsibilities of the leader, therefore, relative to serial discussion are:

1) To verbally define the role of the step as clarification.

2) To pace the group in order to avoid undue argumentation or neglect of some items at the expense of others.

In our training-meeting illustration, the leader would begin by saying:

"Now that we have listed our ideas on the flip chart, I want to take time to go back and briefly discuss each idea.

"The purpose of this discussion is to clarify the meaning of each item on our flip chart. It is also our opportunity to express our understanding of the logic behind the idea, and the relative importance of the item. We should feel free to express varying points of view or to disagree.

"We will, however, want to pace ourselves so that each of the items on the chart receives the opportunity for some attention, so I may sometimes ask the group to move on to further items.

"Finally, let me point out that the author of the item need not feel obliged to clarify or explain an item. Any member of the group can play that role.

[Going to the flip chart, the leader points to item 1.] "Are there any questions or comments group members would like to make about Item 1?"

Generally, groups will spend a little time on each item without much leader intervention once the serial discussion has progressed for a few minutes. It will be quite natural for the group to be a little wordier and discuss early items longer than later items. For example, if the group generates eighteen items, the first six or seven will be discussed longer than the later items. This will not affect final voting so long as the later items are discussed long enough for adequate clarification. People will also become more time conscious as the discussion progresses and more disciplined in avoiding lengthy, nonfunctional discussion.

Where an argument occurs, a leader can intervene by saying: "I think we understand both points of view at this point. Perhaps, however, we should move on to the next item in the interest of time."

Since personal satisfaction is related to the opportunity to discuss items, the leader should not overpace or drive the group through the item list. Groups generally will pace themselves if the leader clearly indicates the available time for this step of the meeting.

Finally, we should note that individuals should not be asked to clarify their own items. Imagine a situation when a subordinate technician listed an item such as: "Inadequate supervisory clarification." Several administrators are present, including his own supervisor. If a group member turns to the author of the item and says: "Joe, what do you mean by that statement?" it could put Joe on the spot. A skillful leader should always intervene and say: "Let's not ask individuals to explain items unless they choose to. Mary, what do the words mean to you?" Although most of the time individuals will volunteer to clarify their own items, the precedent should be established that clarification is a *group* task, not necessarily the unilateral responsibility of the author of the item.

Step 4: Preliminary vote
on item importance

The average NGT meeting will generate over twelve items in each group during its idea-generation phase. Through serial discussion, group members will come to understand the meaning of the item, the logic behind the item, and arguments for and against the importance of individual items. In some manner, however, the group must aggregate the judgments of individual members in order to determine the relative importance of individual items.

Management Science has devoted great effort to determining appropriate mechanisms for aggregating group judgments. It has been shown that the following method increases judgmental accuracy (the ability of a group to arrive at a decision which reflects true group preferences): [3]

1) Having individual members of the group make independent judgments.

2) Expressing these individual judgments mathematically by rank-ordering and/or rating items.

3) Using the mean (x) value of independent judgments as the group's decision.

4) Feeding back the results of individual judgments, talking over these results, and revoting.

The above technique has been used effectively as a voting procedure in NGT. A word about several alternative conventional means for reaching a group decision—consensus, majority rule, and independent listing—will help the reader understand the value of this simple mathematical voting procedure recommended in NGT.

Imagine a group with a list of eighteen items. Thirty minutes remain before the meeting is to adjourn. The group must choose those ideas of greatest merit before concluding the meeting.

Member X feels that Item 13 is very important and speaks forcefully to this point. Member Y feels that Item 13 is not important and also speaks forcefully to this position. The reconciliation of the diverse points of view is complex. Consensus must be achieved through discussion in such a way that the two individuals involved are not offended, too much time is not used, and the cohesion of the group is not disrupted. In the press of time, Member X will be under pressure to modify his or her position and reduce the importance of Item 13 in order to accommodate Member Y. Member Y will conversely be under pressure to change his or her judgment. Thus, consensus may lead to regression toward the mean; in order to maintain group cohesion, individuals may distort their independent judgments to accommodate each other.[4]

3. *Mathematical evidence in support of these propositions is provided in Huber and Delbecq, 1972.*
4. *For a discussion of effective consensus methods and some disadvantages of voting see A. C. Filley,* Interpersonal Conflict Resolution, *in this series.*

Majority rule also distorts judgments. First, the minority position counts for zero. The minority position may be less than 100 percent correct, but counting the position as zero distorts judgment. Further, majority rule may also lead to political maneuvering in order to achieve quorums, bringing into play dynamics separate from judgmental estimates.

Finally, show of hands, open discussion, or other forms of public voting are greatly subject to social pressure. If two high-status members of a six-person group and a third member who is a friend of Member X vote for a particular item, the social pressures are heavy upon Member X to also vote for the item.

Let us look at another alternative voting process, independent listing. In this process, each member of the group writes on a separate sheet of paper the five items that he considers most important. In the case of a flip chart with eighteen items, when the independent listing of each member's priority items is completed, the voting results might be as follows:

ITEM	VOTES
1	2
2	1
3	5
7	5
9	5
10	2
11	1
13	5

Independent listing avoids status, personality, and conformity pressures, and allows each member's vote to influence the group. However, it can be modified to obtain still further information. The listing in the above figure would seem to indicate that items 3, 7, 9, and 13 were the most important. Yet such a process does not yield any measure of degree of importance. Rank-ordering can provide greater information. Imagine that the members were asked to assign a value of 5 to the most important item, and a value of 1 to the least important item. Now the results of the voting are again tallied:

ITEM	VOTES
1	3-2
2	1
3	5-5-4-5-4
7	1-2-1-3-1
9	4-3-2-4-2
10	3-2
11	2
13	1-2-5-5-1

Now it is clear that items 3, 7, 9, and 13, which seemed to be equal in importance when single listing was used, are really very different in importance when ranked.

To summarize, we can increase judgmental accuracy by having group members make individual judgments and express these judgments mathematically. With this brief introduction, we can proceed with a description of a simple voting process often used in NGT meetings.

Step 4 guidelines • The simplest and most often used voting procedure in NGT is a rank-ordering which entails the following leadership steps:

1) Ask the group to select from the entire list of ideas on the flip chart a specific number of "priority" or most important items:

  a. have group members place each priority item on a separate 3 × 5 card.

  b. after members have their set of priority cards, have them rank-order the cards, one at a time.

2) Collect the cards and shuffle them, and record the vote on a flip chart in front of the group.

After a good deal of experimentation, the above steps have been routinized into a simple format. However, they rely heavily on very clear instructions from the leader, so the following guidelines should be read carefully.

The leader begins the voting procedure with a statement as follows:

"We have now completed our discussion of the entire list of ideas, have clarified the meaning of each idea, and have discussed the areas of agreement and disagreement. At this time, I would like to have the judgment of each group member concerning the most important ideas on the list.

"To accomplish this step I wonder if each of you would take five 3 × 5 index cards.

[The leader hands a set of index cards to participants at the table.]

"I would like you to select the five most important items from our list of eighteen items. This will require careful thought and effort on your part.

"As you look at the flip chart sheets and find an item which you feel is very important, please record the item on an index card.

[The leader goes to the flip chart and draws an index card.]

"Please place the number of the item in the upper left-hand corner of the card. For example, if you feel Item 13 is very important, you would write 13 in the upper left-hand corner.

[The leader writes 13 in the upper left-hand corner of the card he has drawn on the flip chart.]

"Then write the identifying words or phrase on the card.

[The leader writes the phrase for Item 13 on the card.]

"Do this for each of the five most important items from our list of eighteen items. When you have completed this task, you should have five cards, each with a separate phrase written on the card, and with identifying numbers using the numbering system from our list of ideas on the flip chart.

"*Do not* rank-order the cards yet. Spend the next few minutes carefully selecting the five cards. We will all rank-order the cards together.

"Are there any questions?"

The leader then proceeds to select five priority cards.

A question comes immediately to mind. Why five cards? As a rule of thumb, individuals are able to accurately rank or rate about seven (± 2) items. That is, group members can select five to nine priority items with some reliability of judgment. We have arbitrarily selected five for our example. Where lists are shorter (around twelve) selecting five priority items is recommended. Where lists are longer (around twenty) selecting eight priority items is desirable. For research purposes, major budgetary meetings, technical meetings, etc., increasing the number of priority items beyond five is desirable.

People easily become confused and use their own numbering system (1 through 5) rather than number the cards in accordance with the numbers on the flip chart, or else write all their ballots on a single card. Using the visual example of an index card drawn on a flip chart helps eliminate confusion.

Some members of the group will complete their selection much quicker than others. When the leader notes that several members have finished voting but others have not, a useful intervention is to say:

> "Some of us have not yet completed our selection of the five most important items. If you have already finished, please take time to recheck to be sure you have made the best selection. Also, let's not disturb those group members who are still making decisions."

In some situations, it is helpful to give the group criteria for choosing the five most important items. This is particularly true where the group composition is somewhat heterogeneous. Examples of criteria are: the five items we should act upon during the next planning period; the five items to which we should allocate our funding; the five items of greatest immediate importance, etc.

After each member of the group has selected five items and written them on separate cards, the leader proceeds as follows:

> "Please spread out your cards in front of you so you can see all five at once. Looking at your set of five cards, decide which one card is the most important. Which card is more important than the other four cards?
>
> [The leader gives the group an opportunity to study their cards.]
>
> "Please write a number 5 in the lower right-hand corner of the card and underline the number three times.
>
> "Turn that card over and look at the remaining four cards. Of the remaining four cards, which is the least important? Write a number 1 in the lower right-hand corner and underline that number three times."

The leader then proceeds to have the group choose the most important of the remaining three cards (number rank 4), the least important of the remaining two cards (number rank 2) and to have the group write number 3 on the last card. Figure 3–3 illustrates a sample index card. The group is given time to reexamine their rank-ordering before passing the cards to the leader. When all the cards are in, the leader shuffles them to preserve anonymity, so that no individual member's voting pattern can be identified.

The procedure of ranking one card at a time is to slow the group members into making careful iterative decisions, rather than hasty decisions. The technique of going from most important to least important is optional but helps maintain interest.

The leader then makes a ballot sheet on a flip chart, numbering the left-hand side of the sheet in accordance with the number of items (e.g., eighteen) from the round-robin listing. He or she then asks one group member to read the item number and the rank number from the stack of voting cards. For example, the index card illustrated

FIGURE 3–3.   Index Card Illustrating Rank-Order Voting Process.

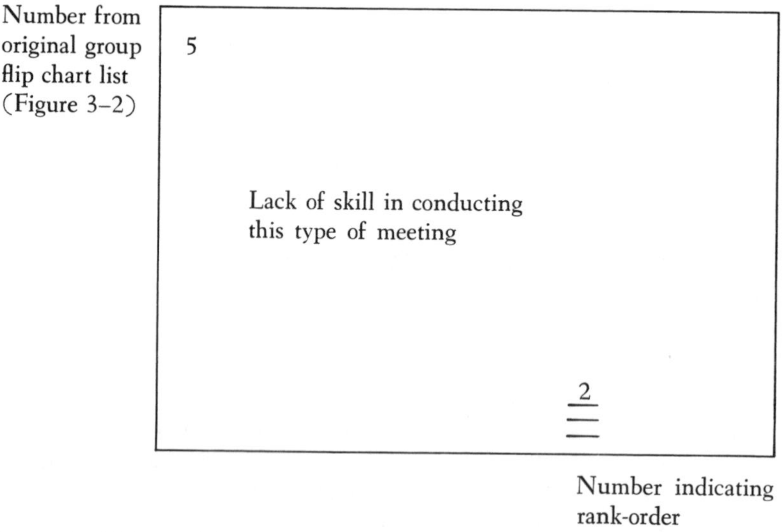

Number from original group flip chart list (Figure 3–2)

5

Lack of skill in conducting this type of meeting

2

Number indicating rank-order

in Figure 3–3 would be read 5–2, meaning Item 5 was ranked 2. With one group member reading and the leader recording, the preliminary vote is tallied as in Figure 3–4.

The reason for underlining the rank number can now be explained. In large groups, individuals will sometimes become confused and write their rank number next to the item number at the top of the card. Unless the rank number is underlined, the person tallying the votes can become confused.

In many situations an NGT meeting will end with Step 4. In other instances where increased judgmental accuracy is desired, two additional steps can be added. These are: discussion of the preliminary vote, and revoting.

FIGURE 3–4.   Voting Tally Sheet on a Flip Chart with Recorded Votes.

————————— Numbers here are rank-order scores of group

1. 3-2-3
2. 2-3-3
3. 2
4. 5-4-5-5
5. 4-4-3
6.
7. 2-2-1-2
8.
9. 1-1
10. 4-4
11. 5-5-1-1-1
12.
13. 1
14.
15.
16.
17.
18. 1-1

——— Numbers in this column correspond to original round-robin listing (Figure 3–2)

Step 5: Discussion of
the preliminary vote

A brief step which can be added to increase judgmental accuracy is a discussion of the preliminary vote as recorded on the flip chart tally (Figure 3–4). The purpose of the discussion is to:

1) Examine inconsistent voting patterns.

2) Provide for the opportunity to rediscuss items which are perceived as receiving too many or too few votes.

If, for example, an item receives a vote of (5–5–3–1–1) there are several possible explanations. Some members of the group may have *information* different from other members. Some members may *understand* the meaning of the item differently from other members. Or, it may simply be that the vote represents a very disperse set of *judgments*. In important situations, it may be worth discussing an item with such split votes, however, to make sure that the differences aren't artificially caused by unequal information, misinformation, or misunderstanding.

It is possible that an item receiving a vote of (5–5) might be discussed by the two members who feel the item is the most important, although no other group members selected it as one of their priority items.

Although discussion prior to revoting seldom results in radical changes, where the judgments of the group are concerned with critical or technical matters, the additional clarification can result in a more accurate final vote.

Step 5 guidelines • The role of the leader in Step 5 is to:

1) Define the task of this discussion as clarification, not social pressure.

2) Ensure that the discussion is brief, so as not to distort perceptions of items not discussed.

Studies of voting show that a three-step process—voting, discussion, revoting—provides a more accurate indication of preferences than voting alone. However, the evidence is somewhat contradictory. Without getting into the scientific debate, we would offer the following speculation: groups who do not talk over votes sometimes make errors due to misinformation, misunderstanding, or unequal information. A brief discussion of the first vote assures that this does not occur. On the other hand, lengthy discussion of earlier judgments can distort group judgment by focusing too much attention on the items discussed as against the total array of items. Thus, in some studies, discussion decreases accuracy. In striking a balance between costs and benefits of discussion and revoting, the way the leader introduces Step 5 and the amount of time devoted to the step are important. With respect to the latter, the discussion of the vote should be short so as not to distort judgments. With respect to role definitions, the following statements at the beginning and end of the discussion are appropriate:

[At the beginning . . .]

"It may be worthwhile to briefly examine the voting pattern in front of us to see if there are any inconsistencies, surprises, or differences members wish to comment on.

"The purpose of this discussion is not to pressure any member to change his or her vote. On the other hand, if we gain additional clarification, some members may wish to modify their original vote."

[At the end . . .]

"Once again, the purpose of this discussion has not been to pressure you to change your original vote. Indeed, you should think carefully before doing so. However, if you honestly have a new perspective as a result of the discussion, you should change your vote."

Step 6: Final vote

Step 6 is the final NGT step. This vote combines individual judgments into a group decision. The final vote:

1) Determines the outcome of the meeting.
2) Provides a sense of closure and accomplishment.
3) Documents the group judgment.

It is possible to follow the same voting procedure as outlined in the discussion of Step 4, the preliminary vote. It is also possible to use more refined voting techniques, such as rating. Moving to a more refined voting procedure depends upon the degree of judgmental accuracy desired, the topic under investigation, and the degree of information possessed by the group. Greater refinement beyond rank-

FIGURE 3–5.   A Rating Form for NGT Final Voting.

No. from flip chart	Item Description	Most Important
		100
———	———————————————————	90
		80
———	———————————————————	70
		60
———	———————————————————	50
		40
———	———————————————————	30
		20
———	———————————————————	10
		0
		Least Important

Instructions

1. Choose the five most important items from the flip chart, and list them in rank-order above.

2. Identify the item by using the number and description from the flip chart.

3. Draw a line from the item to the scale (0-100) at the right, indicating the relative importance of each item.

FIGURE 3–6.   A Rating Form for NGT Final Voting.

No. from flip chart	Item Description	Relative Importance Not important Very important

		0 1 2 3 4 5 6 7 8 9 10
		0 1 2 3 4 5 6 7 8 9 10
		0 1 2 3 4 5 6 7 8 9 10
		0 1 2 3 4 5 6 7 8 9 10
		0 1 2 3 4 5 6 7 8 9 10

Instructions

1. Choose the five most important items from the flip chart, and list them in rank-order above.
2. Identify the items by using the number and description from the flip chart.
3. Rate each item in terms of its importance on the 0-10 scale, with 0 being unimportant, and 10 being very important.

ordering can become specious if individuals are not really able to make fine distinctions. However, as a general rule, the mean (x) of a group's ratings of items on a 0–10 scale or a continuous scale increases the degree of judgmental accuracy where group members are qualified to make more refined distinctions.

Figures 3–5 and 3–6 provide voting forms which are quick and useful ways to obtain mathematical ratings. The group members are first asked to choose (7 ± 2) items as most important. Then, making use of the rating forms in Figures 3–5 and 3–6, members rate the relative importance of the selected priority items.

In summary, if one desires an understanding of the magnitude of differences between priorities, a *rating* of priorities is recommended. (This is particularly true where NGT is used for exploratory research, as discussed in Chapter 5.) On the other hand, if the topic is very general, a simple *reranking* of priorities as in Step 4 may be sufficient.

We have now finished our basic guide to conducting an NGT meeting. Figure 3–7 provides a summary guide of the processes involved.

FIGURE 3–7.   Summary Leadership Guide for Conducting an NGT Meeting.

Design Tasks
 Prepare the NGT Question:
    Staff clarifies objectives
    Illustrates desired items in terms of level of abstraction and scope
    Prepares alternative forms of an NGT question
    Pilot-tests to select the question to be used
 Print the NGT question on nominal group worksheets for each participant.
 Select the voting method suitable to the task. (If ratings are used, prepare rating forms for each participant.)

Preparing the Meeting Room
 Table Arrangement:
    Tables arranged as an open "U" with a flip chart at the open end of the table
    Sufficient space between tables to avoid interference
 Supplies:
    Flip chart for each table and for the leader
    Roll of masking tape
    Nominal worksheets and pencils for each participant
    3 x 5 cards (for ranking); voting forms (for rating)
    Felt pens

Introducing the Meeting
 Welcoming Statement:
    Cordial and warm welcome
    Statement of the importance of the NGT task
    Clarification of the importance of each group member's contribution
    Statement of the use or purpose of the meeting's output

FIGURE 3–7.   (Con't)

Conducting the Nominal Group Process

STEP 1.   SILENT GENERATION OF IDEAS IN WRITING

Process:

Present the nominal question to the group in writing

Verbally read the question

Illustrate level of abstraction and scope desired with example which does not distort (lead) group responses

Avoid other requests for clarification

Charge the group to write ideas in brief phrases or statements

Ask group members to work silently and independently

Model good group behavior

Sanction disruption of the silent, independent activity by comments addressed to group as a whole

Benefits:

Provides adequate time for thinking

Facilitates hard work by the model of other group members reflecting and writing

Avoids interrupting each other's thinking

Avoids premature focusing on single ideas

Eliminates dominance by high-status or aggressive members in idea generation

Keeps the group problem-centered

STEP 2.   ROUND-ROBIN RECORDING OF IDEAS ON A FLIP PAD

Process:

Provide clear instructions concerning the step:

Indicate objective of the step is to map the group's thinking

Explain need to present ideas in brief words or phrases

Explain process of taking one idea serially from each member

Explain group members must decide if items are duplicates

Explain that an individual may "pass" when he has no further items, but may "reenter" later

Express the desirability of hitchhiking and adding new ideas even if they are not on individual nominal worksheets

Explain inappropriateness of discussion prior to completion of listing

Quick, effective mechanical recording:

Record ideas as rapidly as possible

Record ideas in the words used by group members

Provide assistance in abbreviating only in special situations

Make the entire list visible by tearing off completed sheets and taping them on an area visible to all group members

Sanction group as whole if individuals engage in side conversations or attempt to discuss items prior to completing the listing

FIGURE 3–7.   (Con't)

Benefits:

> Equalizes opportunity to present ideas
> Assists in separating ideas from personalities
> Provides a written record and guide:
>> Increases group's ability to deal with a larger number of ideas
>> Avoids loss of ideas
>> Confronts the group with an array of clues
>> Encourages hitchhiking
> Places conflicting ideas comfortably in front of group
> Forces the group to fully explore the problem

STEP 3.   SERIAL DISCUSSION FOR CLARIFICATION

Process:

> Verbally define the purpose of the step:
>> To clarify the meaning of items
>> To explain reasons for agreement or disagreement
> Indicate that final judgments will be expressed by voting so arguments are unnecessary
> Pace the group so that all ideas receive sufficient time for clarification
> Avoid forcing the member who originally lists the idea to be solely responsible for clarifying the item

Benefits:

> Avoids having discussion focus unduly on any particular idea or subset of ideas
> Helps eliminate misunderstanding
> Provides opportunity to express the logic behind items
> Allows members to disagree without argumentation

STEP 4.   PRELIMINARY VOTE ON ITEM IMPORTANCE

Process:

> Ask the group to select from the entire list a specific number (7 ± 2) of priority (important) items:
>> Place each priority item on a separate 3 x 5 card or rating form
>> Rank-order or rate the selected priority items
> Collect the cards or rating forms and shuffle them to retain anonymity
> Tally the vote and record the results on the flip chart in front of the group

Benefits:

> Obtaining independent judgments in writing helps eliminate social pressures
> Expressing judgments mathematically by rank-ordering or rating increases accuracy of judgments
> Displaying the array of individual votes clearly highlights areas needing further clarification or discussion

FIGURE 3–7. (Con't)

STEP 5. DISCUSSION OF THE PRELIMINARY VOTE
Process:
Define the role of the step as clarification, not pressure toward artificial consensus
Keep the discussion brief
Caution group members to think carefully about any changes they make in their voting
Benefits:
Provides group members a final opportunity to clarify their positions
Ensures that "spread" votes really reflect differences in judgment, not unequal information or misunderstanding

STEP 6. FINAL VOTE
Process:
(Repeat Step 4.)
Benefits:
Accurate aggregation of group judgments and error reduction
Closure to the meeting

QUESTIONS FREQUENTLY ASKED ABOUT NGT

Experience in introducing NGT to individuals not familiar with the technique has taught us that there are a number of important questions which the description brings to mind. To conclude the chapter we will raise and answer the questions most frequently asked by individuals when first exposed to NGT.

How many people can participate in an NGT group?

Earlier in this chapter we suggested that an NGT group should be made up of from five to nine members. There are several reasons for this position, drawn from small-group studies concerned with decision making and interaction patterns as well as studies of NGT itself.

First, research focused on decision making shows that a group made up of less than five members lacks resources in terms of the number of critical judgments available to analyze the problem and arrive at a decision. On the other hand, adding beyond ten members often does not increase group accuracy.

Second, in terms of interaction studies, small-group theory suggests the ideal group size is from five to seven. Groups made up of less than five members are less capable of task-oriented discussion due to: (1) overexposure of individual members who have difficulty withdrawing from embarrassing positions; (2) heightened personalization of the discussion; and (3) fewer available members to carry out group roles such as mediator, summarizer, social-emotional supporter, etc. On the other hand, as groups enlarge beyond size seven, satisfaction drops off due to lack of opportunities to participate, the increasing number of members who become inhibited in the presence of many people, the tendency of more aggressive or higher status members to dominate, the tendency of the group to split into subgroups or factions, increased leader dominance, and increased complexity.

Third, the mechanics of NGT become burdensome with a larger group. It simply takes too long to list all the ideas, and too long to discuss each item. Satisfaction drops off as members have less opportunity to participate due to time constraints, and attention spans are stretched beyond capacity due to the large number of items generated.

For all of the above reasons, it is better to divide a ten-person panel into two NGT groups of five persons each, and compare results between the groups as discussed below.

*How can I use the technique, then,
in situations where more than nine persons
need to participate?*

There are many situations where a substantially larger group will be involved in judgmental decision making. For research purposes, a relevant sample is generally much larger than nine individuals. At priority-setting meetings, representative bodies such as boards and commissions often number closer to thirty or forty. NGT can be used in such situations by breaking up the group, adding staff members, and revising Steps 5 and 6.

Imagine a situation where thirty government officials are gathered to utilize NGT in establishing program priorities for a two-year planning period. How might NGT be used for a group of this size?

The group can be divided into five NGT groups of six persons each. Steps 1 through 4 can proceed as outlined in this chapter:

1) Silent generation of ideas.
2) Round-robin recording.
3) Serial discussion.
4) Preliminary vote.

At this point all five groups have ranked the priority program areas they feel should be emphasized during the coming planning period. Ideally, the meeting should be scheduled so that a one and one-half hour luncheon break can be arranged. The recorders from each group, together with staff facilitators, will meet during this luncheon break to create a "master listing" for the entire group of thirty to review and utilize for the final voting in the following manner.

The recorders will have to agree on duplicate priority items (i.e., priority items which the groups identified in common). Each recorder reads the top five (7 ± 2) priorities identified by his or her group, and explains the meaning of the items to the other recorders. After this step, each recorder independently combines duplicate items. Recorders as a group then discuss any disagreements concerning their individual proposals regarding which items should or should not be combined as duplicates.

While the recorders then take time to eat, staff members prepare a carefully worded statement which will convey the accurate meaning for both the combined and individual items. Since group items are often awkwardly written (not a serious problem within a single group since the item is clarified by serial discussion) rewording is often necessary to convey to the entire assembly of thirty the meaning of the item. After the staff has prepared the reworded statements, the recorders as a group edit and revise the wording of the master list. Where items are combined across two or more groups, the number of votes relating to these items must also be combined.

The master list is then typed on a transparency or written on a flip chart with the recorded (combined) vote preceding the wording of the item.

After lunch, the group reassembles as a whole. A staff member leads the entire thirty members in the following steps:

5) Serial discussion of the master list
   a. Clarification

       b. Discussion of the preliminary vote and relative importance

       c. Additions

    6) Final vote

The difference between this serial discussion and Step 5 in our earlier discussion is as follows. Since the master list is not the same as the wording of the earlier individual group items, clarification must precede discussion of the relative importance of items implied by the preliminary vote. After the items on the master list are clarified, the group can discuss the voting results. Groups who were alone in identifying an item will probably want to speak to the relevancy of these items. In addition, concern with perceptions that items were overvalued or undervalued will also be expressed. Finally, there is the possibility that a member of an individual group will ask that an item not placed on the priority list of his group nevertheless be added to the master list. Additions can be accepted and written at the bottom of the master list.

After the discussion, the thirty members as one large group engage in a final vote (rank-ordering and/or rating) and the vote is tabulated and reported.

With this method, one planning agency, using a large support staff and voting on IBM cards which were machine-tabulated, conducted an NGT meeting with six hundred elected officials reviewing priorities concerning land-use planning.

*Should you eliminate duplicate items
on the list of an NGT group
prior to preliminary voting?*

In the above discussion of aggregating the vote across NGT groups to form a master list it was recommended that duplicate items be eliminated by discussion between recorders. The question is often asked if duplicate items should not also be combined before voting within individual NGT groups.

A common sense judgment should be made concerning the level of rigor desired. If NGT is being used for problem identification, then the time necessary to combine duplicate items is probably not worth the effort. For research, technical, or priority-setting purposes, however, it is sometimes desirable to use this additional refinement. Further, technical specialists often feel uncomfortable with an unrefined list in which obvious duplication is present. Thus, there are situations where elimination of duplicate items is desirable.

When should this step take place? *After* serial discussion but *before* preliminary voting.

We can exemplify a useful method for combining items by referring to the list of items in Figure 3–2. Items 1, 5, 14, and 15 all relate to leadership as a potential barrier to conducting an NGT meeting. One possibility would be to try to create a single item such as "lack of necessary leadership skills," representing leadership as a single factor which summarizes all four variants. An alternative would be to rewrite the list, adding the factor title but retaining the individual variants as follows:

A. Lack of necessary leadership skills:
  1. Leader may dominate.
  5. Leader may not be skilled in running the meeting.
  14. Leader may lack sufficient confidence to run the meeting.
  15. Leader may not be sufficiently legitimate to elicit group cooperation.

Such an approach is our preference in combining duplicate items. Why combine the items in this manner?

It seems to us that such an approach avoids two extremes in group voting. First, if the list is not refined, group members could err by placing much of the weight of their voting on several items which are really related to a single factor. Combining related items under a factor title helps alert group members to this problem. A member voting on both 1 and 14 knows he or she is heavily weighing the leadership factor as opposed to another major barrier.

By contrast, simply giving the factor title (A. Lack of leadership skills) leads to two other possible distortions. First, you lose information since it is probably of interest to know which facet of leadership is identified as having greatest salience to the group. Second, an individual may not be able to make as accurate a selection with the general factor label as with the more refined description.

Thus, we favor combining items under major factor titles, with modest rewording of individual items to add clarity if the group wishes to refine its list. A final list would look like this:

A. _____

    1. _____

  12. _____

  23. _____

B. _____

    2. _____

    6. _____

etc.

When such a system is used, members usually vote on numbers only, rather than on the alphabetical factor labels (A, B, C, etc.).

Finally, it should be noted that individuals differ greatly in their ability to rapidly factor and reword. Further, since this is largely a technical task, it does not lend itself to group endeavor. The preferred way to proceed is to have the group break following the listing, and allow capable staff members (or delegate group members) to rework the list. Then, when the group reassembles, it can modify or modestly revise the reworded list before going on to preliminary voting.

Since we are talking about voting,
can you say a little more about
rating versus ranking as a voting procedure?

The recommendation as to when to rank and when to rate depends on the situation and involves several considerations.

One consideration concerns the number of items in the final priority set. If there are just a few, ranking is certainly easier than rating, as it does not require the group members to estimate how much more important each alternative item is than the next most important alternative item. On the other hand, if there are many items, rating is easier since ranking necessarily requires comparing each alternative with all others as yet unranked, and that can involve a very large number of comparisons.

Another consideration concerns accuracy. Rating can provide us with a more accurate indication of an individual's preferences, provided the individual is indeed competent to make fine distinctions.

A final consideration concerns gamesmanship. If members are more interested in getting the group decision to correspond to their individual preferences than they are in obtaining the best group decision, and if they are willing to cheat a little to achieve this, the rating procedure allows them to do so while the ranking procedure does not.

Let us illustrate this by an example. The individual's real preferences for A, B, and C were 4, 2, and 1, respectively. If he really wants the group to choose A, and if he is asked to distribute 100 points across the three alternatives (one approach to rating), he could distribute them 100, 0, and 0 for A, B, and C, instead of 56, 29, and 15 as his true preference would dictate. What he is doing is maximizing the variance among his responses and thus causing his preferences to be more influential than other members whose response variance is less. This could not have occurred if he had to rank the alternatives. A disadvantage of the rating procedure, then, is that it can be manipulated by some members to give themselves more influence than their more honest or less mathematically sophisticated colleagues. There is a trade-off here: rating provides a more accurate indication of an individual's preferences, and therefore can provide us with a more accurate representation of a group's preferences. But it can be manipulated by some members, and thus provide us with a less accurate representation of the group's preferences than would the ranking procedure.

There are three considerations, then, that are involved in choosing between the ranking and rating procedures. One is ease of use, which depends on the number of items to be included in the final priority set. A second consideration is accuracy of our knowledge concerning individual preferences. The last consideration concerns the possibility of gamesmanship. These last two considerations together dictate the accuracy of our knowledge concerning the group's preferences.

How do you write a good NGT question?

NGT is like a microscope. Properly focused by means of a good question, NGT can provide a great deal of conceptual detail about the matter of concern to you. Improperly focused by a poor or misleading question, it tells you a great deal about something in which you are not interested. Therefore, writing the question which is to be the focus of the group's effort is an important preparatory task.

The general process recommended involves the following four steps:

1) Staff discussion of the objective of the NGT meeting.
2) Staff illustration of the type of items sought in terms of:
   a. level of abstraction.
   b. depth versus breadth.

3) Staff development of alternative questions.

4) Pilot-testing alternative questions with a sample group.

It is virtually impossible to frame an NGT question unless there is great clarity about the objective of the meeting. Discussion of the objective in precise terms helps focus attention more clearly on the desired outcome. However, having the staff illustrate the type of items they hope to have listed also is helpful as a second step, since this provides a crosscheck on the stated objective.

A key concern is the level of abstraction and specificity being sought from participants. In general, technical specialists are able to respond in precise technical or scientific language to an NGT question in their field. By contrast, laymen or clients often lack a precise language and respond in generalities. For example, a group of medical doctors responding to a medical diagnosis question will be quite exact in the items which they list. However, when asked to respond outside their technical field on a topic such as "administrative problems" they will resort to generalities such as "poor communication" or "insufficient motivation." Such general responses are next to useless.

As a result, it is particularly important, when asking for responses of nontechnical individuals, or technical individuals outside their own area of speciality, to illustrate the level of abstraction desired. Generally we have found in these situations it is more useful to have the group list critical incidents, examples, or descriptions of behavior than to have them list categories or general problem labels. When you ask an NGT question eliciting this more specific type of response, "poor communication" might become "insufficient information on past medical histories" or "insufficient information about the relative cost of different treatments," which is far more useful.

By illustrating the types of responses sought, the staff can better discover the type of question which will yield these results. Further, they can develop some illustrations to use in clarifying the question with actual NGT participants. However, it is important that the illustrations do not "lead" the group by suggesting actual responses. We have found it helpful to draw illustrations from outside the relevant setting. Thus, if working with airline officials we would use railroad examples which suggest the level of abstraction but do not lead the respondents.

In a similar manner, the group will have to make a decision in terms of breadth versus depth. NGT questions can be formed which drive a group to deep elaboration of a narrow area, or broad conceptually creative exploration of a large area. Again, the staff must be sure of its objectives.

Once the staff is sure of its objectives and of the desired level of abstraction and specificity of response, several (or at least more than one) NGT questions should be composed. These questions should be pilot-tested with a sample group. In the end, a good NGT question is one which evokes the types of responses sought.

A degree of hard work and trial-and-error learning, then, is the secret for writing a successful NGT question.

Can NGT be used where individuals do not have high writing skills?

The above discussion of levels of abstraction, rewording of lists, etc., could easily create the impression that NGT is primarily a technique for professionals with high writing skills. In fact, this is not at all the case.

NGT was originally developed as a technique to facilitate the involvement of disadvantaged citizens in community action agencies under funding by the Office of Economic Opportunity. The entire process, its initial testing, and the early applications were with disadvantaged individuals who would test very low on writing skills. It is a technique used with urban ghetto residents, ADC mothers, rural farmers in Georgia, cub scouts, etc.

Two slight modifications help in using NGT with such populations. First, the leader needs to stress that the independent listing during Step 1—silent generation of ideas in writing—is purely for the individual himself, and that the worksheets will not be collected. This alleviates fear of embarrassment. Second, the recorder will often have to assist participants during Step 2—round-robin listing on a flip chart —to briefly phrase their idea.

Although the prosaic phrasing of professionals may appear more attractive to an outside observer, our experience is that the rougher lists of disadvantaged consumers (which can always be rewritten by staff later) are just as effective in promoting judgmental accuracy.

As a passing note, disadvantaged individuals are particularly enthusiastic about the technique and have very high satisfaction scores, as the NGT meeting is often one of their first experiences where verbal glibness is not the overriding base of power.

How satisfied are individuals
with such a highly structured group process?

There is always a fear that individuals will feel manipulated by or resent the high degree of structure in an NGT meeting. As reported in Chapter 2, this is not the case. Satisfaction scores with NGT are higher than satisfaction scores with the Delphi Technique, and usually slightly higher than scores in conventional discussion meetings. Provided that group members are interested in the topic which is the focus of the meeting, NGT yields high satisfaction scores with the meeting process, the leader, member roles, and meeting outcome.

Occasionally, individuals who have a high need for dominance and/or are of high status are threatened by the technique, as they correctly perceive that they cannot manipulate the meeting. Generally, once they have sufficient experience with the technique and discover the high quality of outcome, their fears are alleviated. Instances of individuals feeling threatened, however, are very rare and occur with no more frequency than with the use of other techniques.

People often ask if experience with NGT wears thin in the sense that repeating the process is less successful. Usually the opposite occurs. As individuals become familiar and comfortable with the technique, they use it with greater frequency where it is an appropriate group process.

How can I be sure
that the decisions arrived at in an NGT meeting
will be accepted by the rest of the organization
or other groups?

You can't. NGT is no different from any other group process in that sense. Decisions arrived at have to be judged by both acceptability and quality. Used appropriately and with a properly composed group, NGT will help assure quality of judgments. Organizational acceptance is based on many variables of which quality is but one. Within the group itself, however, NGT processes yield high member acceptance of outcomes.

Won't high-status and more extroverted individuals
still dominate Step 3—serial discussion—
and Step 5—discussion of the preliminary vote?

High-status and extroverted individuals will speak more than other group members during these steps. However, our research shows that independent voting allows group members to choose outcomes other than those preferred by the more verbally dominant. Indeed, while there is a high correlation between amount of talking and influence over outcome in discussion groups, this is not necessarily the case in NGT. NGT group members may not be willing to out-talk or argue with verbally prominent members, but with independent voting they can vote away from the position of verbally prominent members.

On the other hand, where the amount of talking is related to the degree of expertise, which is often the case, NGT members will vote for ideas espoused by more expert members. The point, then, is that logical arguments are listened to, but high verbiage cannot control behavior as it does in the interacting group.

Our data also clearly shows that NGT outcomes are not dependent on the frame of reference of the group leader. The leader is a full participant in the NGT meeting in the sense that he or she is also free to contribute ideas. Thus, leaders are not excluded or muffled in any way in NGT, but they cannot overcontrol outcomes. By contrast, most interacting groups seldom break outside the frame of reference of the leader.

Who should be invited to participate in an NGT meeting?

NGT is like a vacuum. It is a powerful means to draw out the insight and information possessed by group members. However, if there is nothing to "draw out" even a powerful vacuum is useless. Thus, to say NGT is a superior judgmental group process presupposes that we are comparing groups made up of equally competent individuals using different processes.

No group process is a substitute for appropriate membership. Group processes simply facilitate the decoding of ideas once the proper individuals are assembled.

In Chapter 5 when we discuss different utilizations of NGT in research, planning, and proposal review situations we will be more explicit about group composition for those specific purposes. For the moment, a broad generalization is that group members must be interested in the problem and have either experience or education which makes them a resource to the group in dealing with the problem at hand. Finally, group members should be sufficiently flexible so as to be able to openly explore various points of view.

One also has to consider whether to form a heterogeneous (multiple ages, disciplines, positions) or homogeneous group. This issue was taken up in the theoretical discussion in Chapter 2. Heterogeneous groups are generally more creative, but communication difficulties emerge. As a simple rule of thumb, individuals must be able to speak a common "language." For example, placing medical doctors and uninitiated patients in the same group generally is a poor strategy. Medical jargon will mystify the patients. It would be better to form one NGT group made up of doctors, and one group made up of patients, and then to compare results between groups. On the other hand, mixing a psychologist with a sociologist and an anthropologist generally works well since they can speak the common language of the behavioral sciences.

What skills must the leader possess
to overcome resistance to an unfamiliar technique?

The leader must: (1) understand the process; (2) possess self-confidence to lead a group through the process steps; and (3) be legitimate so as to be accepted as he or she directs group behavior.

An individual who has read this chapter and has had the opportunity to participate in an NGT training meeting normally adequately understands the process. Self-confidence is largely a function of additional opportunities to practice the technique under "safe" (not tense or controversial) circumstances. We would encourage individuals familiarizing themselves with any new group process to practice the process on relevant but less significant problems prior to leading a meeting of high-status individuals around a pivotal issue.

Legitimacy has to be defined relative to the reference group and the status order within the reference group. A white teacher in a predominantly black central city school is probably a poor leader for a faculty NGT group. A female nurse is probably a poor leader for a male research medical staff. The obvious criteria that allow an individual to exercise leadership, elicit cooperation, and specify group processes for any meeting apply to the leadership of NGT groups.

If the three conditions of skill, self-confidence, and legitimacy are present, then the leader will not find it necessary to engage in any elaborate justifications for each step of NGT. Instead, he can simply ask the group to begin by . . . (and describe Step 1)—then proceed to . . . (and describe Step 2), etc.

There is one exception to this generalization. If group members are attending a conference as experts and have a preconception about how the meeting will proceed, or expect to have the opportunity for dialogue, etc., then some justification for using NGT is necessary. A brief statement of the objectives of the meeting and a brief theoretical explanation of the NGT process is appropriate in such situations.

What are the disadvantages of the NGT process and when should it not be used?

NGT is only one of many important group processes which skilled managers should know. Since it is a special-purpose group process, it is easy to specify the circumstances when the technique is useful. NGT is an appropriate group process: (1) to identify elements of a problem situation; (2) to identify elements of a solution program; and (3) to establish priorities; where the judgments of several individuals must be decoded and aggregated into a group decision. Thus, the common element of each of these three applications is that the decision-making situation is complex, and calls for the pooling or aggregation of individual judgments. For routine meetings, where the focus is on information exchange and coordination, other leader-centered meeting formats are appropriate. Where the purpose of the meeting is to bring together a group for negotiation or compromise, bargaining techniques are useful. Finally, for policy setting in a representative body, parliamentary procedure and its variants are appropriate. Likewise, there are other creative problem-solving techniques: conventional brainstorming, consensus, and integrative decision making, for example.

Even in the three most typical applications for NGT—problem identification, solution exploration, and priority setting—there are occasions when NGT would not be appropriate. NGT takes considerable time, usually sixty to ninety minutes. There are occasions when a less precise but speedier process is necessary. Likewise, NGT calls for certain physical facilities and leadership requirements which are not always present. Finally, the technique can deal with only one question at a time, so that NGT is a single-purpose technique. Also, NGT is inappropriate for simpler problems which can be resolved in a less structured interacting group.

During the last several years, NGT has been widely utilized in complex program-planning situations in health, education, welfare, and industry. In particular, it has been widely adopted as an exploratory research technique for problem exploration, as a priority-setting technique, as a meeting format wherein experts come together to explore component parts of a solution, and as a proposal review technique. Each of these four specific applications will be discussed in Chapter 5.

REFERENCES

Huber, George, and A. L. Delbecq. "Guidelines for Combining the Judgments of Individual Group Members in Decision Conferences." *Academy of Management Journal,* 15, 2 (June 1972).

The Delphi Technique

4

Delphi is a group process which utilizes written responses as opposed to bringing individuals together. Like NGT, it is a means for aggregating the judgments of a number of individuals in order to improve the quality of decision making. Because Delphi does not require face-to-face contact, however, it is particularly useful for involving experts, users, resource controllers, or administrators who cannot come together physically. Delphi, unlike NGT, lets people remain anonymous but, like NGT, prevents domination by certain individuals. Delphi can also be used to aggregate judgments where people are hostile toward one another, or where individual personality styles would be distracting in a face-to-face setting.

Delphi is essentially a series of questionnaires. The first questionnaire asks individuals to respond to a broad question. (Delphi questions might focus upon problems, objectives, solutions, or forecasts.) Each subsequent questionnaire is built upon responses to the preceding questionnaire. The process stops when consensus has been approached among participants (Dalkey, 1967), or when sufficient information exchange has been obtained.

HOW HAS DELPHI BEEN USED?

Delphi has been employed in many different settings. Originally it was used as a process for technological forecasting (Helmer, 1967; Pyke and North, 1969). For example, Delphi has been used to obtain predictions concerning the impact of a new land-use policy upon population growth, pollution, agriculture, taxes, etc. (Kaufman and Gustafson, 1973).

However, its applications have broadened beyond technological forecasting so that Delphi, like NGT, has become a multiple-use planning tool. For example, Delphi has been used to alert participants to recent scientific advances. Since articles are frequently behind actual research at the time of printing, Delphi can provide a more updated exchange of scientific or technical information than a literature search by drawing upon the *current* knowledge of experts. In this manner, Delphi has been used to evaluate strengths and weaknesses of information systems relative to developmental planning (Turoff, 1971).

Like NGT, Delphi can be used to help identify problems (Wisconsin Governor's Health Task Force, 1973), set goals and priorities, and identify problem solutions. It can also be used to clarify positions and delineate differences among diverse reference groups. In this latter sense, Delphi can be an important preconference planning technique. Frequently groups are asked to attend a conference to resolve differences between them concerning important issues. However, such a forum is often ineffective since it is not predicated on a clear understanding of the alternate views of each reference group. Delphi can be used prior to the conference to delineate a variety of positions.

From these examples, it can be seen that Delphi can be applied to a wide range of program-planning and administrative concerns.

WHEN SHOULD DELPHI NOT BE USED?

There are three critical conditions necessary to complete a successful Delphi:

1) Adequate time.
2) Participant skill in written communication.
3) High participant motivation.

Delphi should not be used when time is limited. Most Delphi studies take more than a month to implement. As a rule of thumb, the minimal required time for a Delphi is about 45 days (see Table 4-1). Delphi should likewise not be used with groups that have difficulty in reading or in expressing themselves in written communication. Finally, like all other group processes, the quality of responses is very much influenced by the interest and commitment of the participants. Delphi requires especially high participant motivation since other people are not present to stimulate and maintain motivation.

PARTICIPANTS IN DELPHI

In most Delphi situations, three different groups of people will carry out the process: (1) the top management decision makers who will utilize the outcomes of the Delphi study; (2) the professional staff member together with his support team; and (3) the respondents to the Delphi questionnaire whose judgments are being sought.

Decision makers

Delphi is a tool to aid understanding or decision making. Therefore, Delphi will be an effective process only if those decision makers who will ultimately act upon the results of the Delphi are actively involved throughout the process. Consequently, a *work group* of five to nine members, composed of both staff and decision makers, is normally formed to conduct the Delphi process. This work group will develop and analyze all questionnaires, appraise the utility of the information obtained, and revise the questionnaires if they are not effective.

Staff

A professional staff member who can guide the work group through the process is a critical element in conducting a Delphi study. This person should have experience in designing and conducting Delphi studies. It is also helpful if the staff member is knowledgeable about the problem area or issue being studied. In addition, support staff is also needed to do such things as type and send questionnaires, receive and do some preliminary processing of results, and schedule meetings.

Respondents

Respondents are those people whose judgments are being sought, and who agree to answer the questionnaires. While decision makers and staff can't select the respondent panel until the problem is precisely formulated, identifying available qualified people is a critical prerequisite for a successful Delphi.

THE DELPHI PROCESS

Table 4–1 outlines the various steps involved in the Delphi process, and the minimum amount of time required for each step. We will discuss each step in turn below.

1) Develop the Delphi question

This is the key to the Delphi process. If respondents do not understand the initial broad question which is the focus of the Delphi Technique, they may answer inappropriately or become frustrated with the questionnaire and lose interest. We have found that three to four hours are often required to formulate the Delphi question precisely.

Staff should interview the decision makers to clarify exactly what information is desired, and how the information will be used. It often takes an hour or more for staff to arrive at a clear sense of the exact type of responses decision makers want from respondents. Frequently the decision makers' final Delphi question is quite different from their initial question.

To illustrate this first step, imagine that decision makers have requested a Delphi study to evaluate the usefulness of the Delphi Technique in program planning. In this illustration, staff might find that the decision makers first talked about desiring the Delphi study in order to identify areas where Delphi could be used as a planning aid. After some discussion, however, it may become clear that decision makers are already well informed on this subject and that their real concern is to get a balanced picture of the strengths and weaknesses of Delphi as a means for assessing community needs and establishing priorities. Thus, it is important that staff take care in formulating the Delphi question.

Key questions staff should ask decision makers in question

TABLE 4–1.   Process Outline and Schedule for Delphi.

Activities	Estimated Minimum Time for Accomplishment
1) Develop the Delphi question	½ day
2) Select and contact respondents	2 days
3) Select sample size	½ day
4) Develop Questionnaire #1 and test	1 day
a. Type and send out	1 day
b. Response time	5 days
c. Dunning time (if used)	3 days
5) Analysis of Questionnaire #1	½ day
6) Develop Questionnaire #2 and test	2 days
a. Type and send out	1 day
b. Response time	5 days
c. Dunning time (if used)	3 days
7) Analysis of Questionnaire #2	1 day
8) Develop Questionnaire #3 and test	2 days
a. Type and send out	1 day
b. Response time	5 days
c. Dunning time (if used)	3 days
9) Analysis of Questionnaire #3	1 day
10) Prepare a final report	4 days
a. Type report and send out	1 day
b. Prepare respondents' report	1 day
c. Type report and send out	1 day
Total estimated minimum time	44½ days

formulation are: Why are you interested in this study? What do you need to know that you don't know now? And most importantly— how will results from the Delphi influence decision making once the study is completed?

2) Select and contact respondents

Who should constitute the respondent panel in a Delphi study? It is unrealistic to expect effective participation unless respondents: (1) feel personally involved in the problem of concern to the decision makers; (2) have pertinent information to share; (3) are motivated to include the Delphi task in their schedule of competing tasks; and (4) feel that the aggregation of judgments of a respondent panel will include information which they too value and to which they would not otherwise have access.

Items 1 and 2 above suggest that participants must have a deep interest in the problem and important knowledge or experience to share. (As will be discussed in Chapter 5, different respondents are required depending on whether the objective of the Delphi is to identify problems, in which case users and field staff may be selected, or to identify components of creative solutions, in which case specialists, experts, and administrators may be selected.) The key point is to identify the qualifications of desirable respondents.

Once the general characteristics of desired respondents are agreed upon, a *nomination process* should be used to select specific individual respondents. In other words, the work group should first identify target groups likely to possess relevant information or experience concerning the objectives toward which decision makers are aiming the Delphi. Then staff should solicit nominations of well-known and respected individuals from members within the target groups if the Delphi is aimed at experts, or an appropriate random sample of respondents if "representativeness" is a criterion.[1] Even when a nonrandom response panel is chosen, one should ask for nominations from a large and diverse set of target group members in order to minimize distortion in the data. Since Delphi requires considerable participant effort, the procedure of selecting respondents through nomination can also increase motivation, since there is a degree of flattery associated with being nominated to be an "expert" respondent.

Items 3 and 4 (motivation and interest in outcome) are often established in initial contacts with potential participants. Participants must be convinced of the importance of the Delphi's objectives and the importance of their participation. Each potential respondent should be contacted by telephone or face to face by someone whom the respondent respects. The contact person should clearly describe the objectives of the Delphi study, the nature of the respondent panel, the obligations of participants, the length of time the Delphi process will take, and the information that will be shared among participants. Only after a de-

---

1. *Obviously, nonrandom nominations violate sampling procedures. However, a crosscheck of the representativeness of a Delphi questionnaire outcome can be tested by follow-up research utilizing a simplified survey research questionnaire format. The follow-up questionnaire can provide for adequate response ratios of randomly selected participants.*

tailed and personal introduction will most respondents participate fully
in the Delphi process.

3) Select sample size

The size of the respondent panel is variable. With a homogeneous group of people, ten to fifteen participants might be enough.
However, in cases where various reference groups are involved, several
hundred people might participate. Our experience indicates that few
new ideas are generated within a homogeneous group once the size
exceeds thirty well-chosen participants. However, there may be good
reasons for selecting a larger number of respondents. If the purpose
of the Delphi study involves increasing group understanding or gaining
group support, then a large panel of participants might be involved
simply for motivational as opposed to informational purposes.

Remember, however: the more people that are involved, the
more effort that is needed for analysis. Therefore, staff would do well
to hold the number of participants in the Delphi study to a minimally
sufficient number of respondents and seek verification of results through
follow-up survey research.

To continue our earlier illustration, where decision makers are
seeking to study the strengths and weaknesses of using Delphi for
planning, our work group decides they want input, by means of the
questionnaire, from theoretical experts on group process techniques.
They also want to hear from proponents of Delphi who have used the
technique successfully in program planning, and opponents who have
tried the technique and were not successful in utilizing it for program
planning. Three individuals are used to nominate respondents: a
prominent researcher who helped develop the Delphi Technique, a
governmental staff person who wrote a review paper describing the
uses of the technique for planning, and a sociologist who has written
highly critical articles concerning Delphi.

Each nominator is contacted by phone and asked to suggest
names of people who should either be part of the respondent panel,
or who can nominate other people as potential respondents. Two of
three nominators also suggest themselves as participants. The final
respondent panel consists of forty-eight names, including two of the
three nominators.

Each member of the work group selects six potential respondents
to contact. By telephone, they describe the Delphi study and invite the

people to participate as members of the respondent panel. As mentioned above, at this time they stress the study's purpose, describe why it is important, indicate the unique qualifications which have been ascribed to the potential respondent, suggest why he or she ought to participate, tell what will be required of respondents, and indicate how results will be disseminated among respondents.

Thirty of the forty-eight people agree, but only five of the thirty are opponents of Delphi. The decision makers discuss this imbalance and agree that they want a minimum of fifteen opponents. Nominators are contacted once again to obtain more names of potential respondents, and the process continues until the requisite number of opponents agree to participate.

4) Develop Questionnaire #1 and test

The first questionnaire in a Delphi allows participants to write responses to a broad problem issue.[2] The benefits of this step include some of the benefits of NGT as discussed in Chapters 2 and 3, plus others:

1) Adequate time for thinking and reflection.
2) Avoidance of undue focusing on a particular idea.
3) Avoidance of competition, status pressures, and conformity issues.
4) The benefit of remaining problem-centered.
5) Avoidance of choosing between ideas prematurely.

(but unique to Delphi):

6) Flexibility in allowing participants to respond at the most convenient time.
7) No travel time required.
8) Anonymity.

2. As Delphi is being described in this chapter, it is being utilized as a pilot research instrument. As such, the first question is broad, and participants create subcategories and variables themselves. Other utilizations of Delphi can approximate survey research, where the variables are already developed, and concern is only with refinement and movement toward consensus concerning the relative importance of individual variables.

Unlike NGT, where staff are present at a meeting with participants, in the Delphi Technique the cover letter and questionnaire are the only means by which the work team can facilitate these benefits. Consequently, it is crucial that these materials be well prepared. The cover letter should include the following elements: thanking the individual for participating, explaining why his or her help is needed, explaining how the results of the Delphi will be utilized, and providing instructions and a response date. Figure 4–2 offers one example of such a letter.

The first questionnaire can take several forms, but in program planning it would most likely be one or two rather open-ended questions. For example, in our illustrative Delphi, the participants might respond to a problem statement such as that illustrated in Figure 4–3.

FIGURE 4–2.   Letter for Questionnaire #1.

Dear:

Thank you for agreeing to participate in our analysis of the potential benefits from using the Delphi Techniques in program planning. Your insights will be most helpful in evaluating the applications of this tool.

Specifically, we need your help to identify and explore the principle strengths and weaknesses of Delphi as it applies to program planning.

The results will be used by key executives in the following agencies to determine whether to utilize Delphi for planning: . . . In addition, each of you will receive a critique of the benefits and difficulties of the Delphi process as applied for this purpose.

I am attaching the first in a series of questionnaires designed to seek your assistance to clarify these issues. Please complete the enclosed questionnaire and return it to us in time for analysis on (date) . Again, thank you for your help.

Sincerely,

FIGURE 4–3.

Questionnaire #1

Please list the major strengths and weaknesses of the Delphi process
as an aid to program planning. Please be clear and concise.

STRENGTHS   WEAKNESSES

Signature _____
(Optional)

One frequent modification to such a format would be a request
to "cite an example from your own personal experience to illustrate
each strength or weakness identified." This can help clarify the meaning
of otherwise obscure responses, but it does significantly increase the
participants' work load.

Mechanics • The following points are important in making the first questionnaire a success:

1) Be sure both the letter and the questionnaire contain no technical errors. Don't jeopardize your rapport with respondents by misspelling a word or a name.

2) Make the letter no more than one page long. The respondents are busy people who will be bored with rhetoric.

3) Send a personally typed rather than a xeroxed letter. Seek the help of a graphic artist or printer to make the questionnaire visually attractive.

4) Be sure the task instructions are clear and that they have been tested, just as the Delphi question has been.

5) Simplify return of the questionnaire by means of a self-addressed, stamped envelope.

6) Send out the first questionnaire the same day a person agrees to participate. Delay may cause respondents to lose their enthusiasm for the project. If they receive a letter the day after you call, you will impress upon respondents the sincerity of your interest in their participation.

7) Fix a specific deadline (normally two weeks) for receipt of the response.

Even when all the above concerns have been carefully attended to, some participants will not respond unless they receive further encouragement. Two forms of encouragement seem to be successful, and sometimes both may be needed. One is the "dunning letter," to be sent one week after the first questionnaire is sent. Along with reminding respondents of the deadline date, it should also offer to answer any questions by collect telephone contact. For those people who still do not respond, a further step may have to be taken. Respondents are telephoned to see if they are having any problem with the questionnaire, and reminded of how much their input is needed.

5) *Analysis of Questionnaire #1*

At this stage of the Delphi study, questionnaires have been sent to and returned by respondents. The analysis of the questionnaire should result in a summary list of items identified and comments made. The list should reflect the initial opinions of respondents concerning key variables, yet be short enough for all respondents to easily review, criticize, support, or oppose. The analysis of Questionnaire #1 proceeds as follows.

A meeting of the work group (decision makers and staff) is called. Each member of the work group should have the following materials available to him at the meeting:

1) Copies of each variable or item from every Delphi questionnaire.[3]

2) A pad of paper.

3) Tape.

4) Pencils.

5) Scissors.

In addition, the room should have one flip chart, felt pens, and a roll of masking tape. Coffee, tea, etc., should be available. The meeting room should be large enough so that each person has at least a 30 x 60-inch desk area available.

Each work group member sorts his or her cards (each card representing one item from one questionnaire) so that essentially identical items are placed in a stack. In other words, items stacked together should say about the same thing, even though expressed in different ways. Then each group member labels each card stack.

For example, suppose three Delphi respondents suggested: "Delphi studies take too long"; "Be sure at least seventy days are available for the study"; "If you want results in a couple of weeks, forget it."

These three response cards would be stacked together. A label such as "Delphi studies require at least seventy days to complete" might identify the card stack.

Next, all members of the work group must agree on a set of labels suitable for coding all responses. The process for arriving at agreement on labels is as follows: each member lists his or her labels on a flip chart. One person then uses this list to create a single list.

3. *Each item identified by respondents should be placed on a separate 3 × 5 card. Comments elaborating on an item should be placed on the card containing the item. If card preparation is impossible, questionnaires can be cut into strips, with each strip containing an individual item on a questionnaire. The strips can then be duplicated for each member of the work group.*

The group discusses and modifies the single list and agrees upon a final list of labels. The essential criterion for establishing the list is to arrive at a mutually exclusive but exhaustive set of categories. Each final label must be clear and concise.

The next step is to divide the work group into two-person teams. Each team is assigned a separate set of labels and must transform the labels into complete sentences which are easily understood. These sentences will be the content items for Questionnaire #2.

Before leaving the meeting the work group should schedule meetings for analyzing all future questionnaires to ensure that time is set aside for questionnaire analysis. The legitimacy of a Delphi study depends upon each iterative questionnaire being ready and sent to participants on time. Thus, the work group must meet promptly upon receipt of each questionnaire.

Sample analysis of Questionnaire #1 • A second and simple Delphi illustration may be useful in discussing the analysis of Questionnaire #1.

Suppose a group of entrepreneurs have contacted you to conduct a Delphi study that would help them build a new car wash system which could compete successfully in the market. The decision makers are two financiers, one marketing expert, and two gas station operators who will manage and operate the system. They have agreed that in order to compete successfully they must develop a system that eliminates many of the problems prevalent in existing car washes. More than that, the marketing expert feels that including potential clients in the design of this system will offer a unique opportunity to develop market loyalty and provide a useful sales pitch for other potential clients. The decision makers chose the Delphi Technique because they see a need for involving a wide range of people, particularly consumers. Because of the importance of the effort itself, they have agreed to commit the necessary time to development and analysis of questionnaires and exploration of the results obtained. They have hired you and then suggest persons as staff for the Delphi project.

The first questionnaire to be sent to the one hundred consenting participants asked respondents to identify the principal barriers faced in obtaining a good car wash. Eighty-five returns were obtained. As the work group sorts the responses they agree that the items can be classified under the following labels: (1) cost; (2) speed; (3) attitude; (4) quality; (5) access; and (6) other factors.

Within the various card stacks are statements like:

"The car wash is never open when I want to use it."

"I am too busy to take time to get the car washed."

"The car wash is too far away."

"There is never a car wash around when you need one."

"It takes me forty minutes just to drive to and from the car wash. In that time I can do it myself."

"I do a lot of traveling. I must keep my car clean but it's hard to find someone who will wash my car when I need it."

"There are only two places in this whole town that will wash my car."

Further analysis through discussion results in consensus by the work group that three points are being made:

1) The car wash is *not open* when the client has time to use it (hours).
2) It takes *too long* to get a car wash (access time).
3) The client has *trouble finding* a car wash when he/she needs it (identification).

These three items will be included in the contents of Questionnaire #2.

6) Develop Questionnaire #2 and test

It is important that each item in Questionnaire #2 accurately conveys the meaning which respondents attempted to communicate by means of Questionnaire #1. This implies a pretest of Questionnaire #2, just as there needs to be a pretest of Questionnaire #1. Pretests can be accomplished by a pilot test prior to mailing the questionnaires, with a sample of respondents not part of the formal respondent panel.

Questionnaire #2 asks participants to review the items identified in Questionnaire #1 as summarized by the work group, argue in favor of or against those items, and clarify items. It also has participants rank items to establish preliminary priorities among the items. The benefits of Questionnaire #2 are:

1) Areas of disagreement are identified.
2) Areas of agreement are identified.
3) Items requiring clarification are identified and discussed.
4) An early understanding of priorities emerges.

A few comments relative to these benefits may help.

Disagreement: The items in Questionnaire #2 indicate the initial positions of participants. Comments and reactions to the items can further clarify those positions. Based on this information, the analysis of Questionnaire #2 can indicate, to some degree, why differences in positions occur.

Agreement: The comments and priority voting indicate those areas where consensus is already clear. This permits the work group to begin to consider decisions which can be addressed even before the final questionnaire of the Delphi study is completed.

For example, using the first Delphi illustration concerned with planning, suppose that one of the issues that all respondents to our Delphi agree upon is that a Delphi takes too long. Without waiting for further questionnaire results, the decision makers and staff can search for ways to cope with that time requirement. For example, they can explore the possibility of reducing time by using computers to communicate with participants.

Clarification: Items on Questionnaire #2 where respondents are unclear as to the meaning will be identified. Then in Questionnaire #3 the item can be reconstructed in collaboration between staff and respondents so that misunderstandings do not distort final voting.

Understanding: Questionnaire #2 is the beginning of a dialogue between participants. Questions can be raised. Statements of support and criticism can be made. Results will be relayed to all participants through Questionnaire #3, allowing respondents to consider these further clarifications and vote more accurately. The intent is to help participants understand each others' position and to move toward accurate judgments concerning the relative importance of items.

Mechanics • The mechanics of the second questionnaire follow those of the first: a letter, a self-addressed envelope, and a questionnaire are sent to each respondent.

The format for Questionnaire #2 should accomplish four things:

1) It should be easy to identify and understand the items taken from Questionnaire #1.

2) It should be easy to add comments of agreement, disagreement, or clarification.

3) It should have clear and simple voting instructions.

4) It should be short enough to complete in twenty to thirty minutes.

An illustration of Questionnaire #2 is given in Figure 4-4. Some further elaboration about the format is in order.

Ease of understanding: Items should be presented in full sentences with key words underlined. The ordering of the statements is a matter of personal preference.

Ease of commenting and voting: Ample room should be left for comments of agreement, disagreement, or clarification. The place for a vote should be clearly marked. The task statement should be clear.

Time: Test the questionnaire to be sure it can be completed in less than thirty minutes. If it is too long, find some way to reduce the time involved. Possibilities include shortening the number of items, making it easier to read, and enlisting professional graphic arts assistance in terms of layout.

Task Statement • In Questionnaire #2, participants are asked to do three things: (1) review the list of items and comment on them; (2) vote for the most important items; and (3) return the questionnaire by a particular date. Sometimes the task statement or instructions are printed in full on a cover sheet and in summary form on the questionnaire itself. An example of a task statement follows:

1) Review all items on the questionnaire. Comment on any items you wish. Feel free to ask questions, make clarifications, argue in favor of or against items. Brevity and clarity will facilitate our analysis.

2) Select the ten items you feel are most important. Assign a value of "10" to the most important. Assign a value of "9" to the next most important, and so on, until the tenth item (the least important of the ten) is assigned a value of "1". Note

FIGURE 4–4.

$\qquad$ *QUESTIONNAIRE* #2 $\qquad$ Code $\underline{\hspace{2cm}}$

Instructions: Please review each of the following items identified in Questionnaire #1 as important barriers to obtaining a car wash. If you wish to add comments expressing agreement, disagreement, or clarification concerning the item, please do so in the space provided. Also feel free to add items. Finally, please rank-order the ten most important items as you perceive them at this time.

Priority Vote	Items from Questionnaire #1	Comments on Items	agree disagree clarify
_____	1) The car wash is *not open* when the client has time to use it (hours)		
_____	2) It takes *too long* to get a car wash (access time)		
	etc.		
_____	19) The client has *trouble finding* a car wash when he/she needs it (identification)		
	Additional items:		
_____	20)		
_____	21)		

---

that this is merely a preliminary vote. You will have the opportunity to revote in Questionnaire #3.

3) Return your response in the enclosed self-addressed, stamped envelope by $\underline{\hspace{2cm}}$ (date).

Cover Letter • The cover letter should include items similar to those in Questionnaire #1. It should thank the participants for their responses, express continued need for their help, and indicate the purpose of Questionnaire #2 and its place in relation to Questionnaire #3. It should also review the Delphi question and give the participants some feeling that the study is proceeding properly ("Over 90 percent of the participants responded to the last questionnaire. This is very encouraging.").

The same suggestions for ensuring a good response rate hold for this questionnaire as for Questionnaire #1. Use a "dunning" letter about one week after the questionnaire is sent. Place phone calls to those people who do not respond or whose participation is particularly vital. Above all, however, be sure you mail the questionnaire on schedule. Don't let people forget they are involved in an important study. Show that you are concerned enough to be on time.

7) *Analysis of Questionnaire #2*

The analysis of Questionnaire #2 should: (1) tally votes for items; and (2) summarize comments made about the items in a form that is both thought-provoking and easy to understand.

Each member of the work group should have the following materials at the analysis meeting:

1) Copies of each response to Questionnaire #2.[4]
2) Pad of paper.
3) Tape.
4) Pencils.
5) Scissors.
6) Vote tally sheet.

The *vote tally sheet* shows the total votes received by each item and also how respondents differed in their votes. (The tally sheet can be compiled as responses come in.) The format for the tally sheet is shown in Figure 4–5.

The benefits of the vote tally sheet are that the votes are displayed in a manner that permits the work group to see not only the total vote, but also (1) the number of people voting for an item; and (2) the diversity of rankings assigned to an item by respondents. This

4. *Items do not need to be placed on 3 × 5 cards for this analysis. Copies of the responses and comments are sufficient.*

FIGURE 4–5.   Tally Sheet for Questionnaire #1 Rankings.

ITEM	NUMBER OF RESPONDENTS VOTING FOR ITEM	INDIVIDUAL VOTES	TOTAL VOTE
1)	7	10–9–10–9–6–9–10	63
2)	6	8–6–8–5–8–6	41
3)	3	10–9–10	29
4)	4	7–6–7–8	28
5)	5	1–2–1–5	9
6)	1	2	2
etc.			

information is valuable for several reasons. Work group members may wish to contact a respondent who voted for an item receiving no other votes to obtain an explanation for the next questionnaire as to why he or she felt the item was important. The work group may also wish to look at backgrounds of respondents to see if the ranking patterns can be related to reference group characteristics.

The *total vote* for an item is obtained by adding the individual ranks assigned to items. Thus, if Item #1 received ranks of 10–9–10–9–6–9–10 (10 being most important and 1 being least important), the total vote would be 63. Note the value of asking your respondents to rank-order items by assigning the *largest* number to the most important item.

If there are a large number of participants, it will be difficult to include all comments in Questionnaire #3. Once again, the work group can sort items so that all comments related to a given item are in the same stack, and assign a label to the stack. It is also possible to condense the comments even further by writing one-paragraph summaries analyzing the comments. Such a paragraph might start by saying: "In general, respondents seem to feel that . . . ." The advantage of the summary paragraph is that it makes Questionnaire #3 easier to read. The disadvantage is that such paragraphs increase the chance of either misinterpreting or neglecting a respondent's comments. Thus it is important to carefully compare the final summary statements or paragraphs to be used in Questionnaire #3 to the original comments taken from Questionnaire #2.

As an illustration, let's return to our second Delphi example, the car-wash study. A typist would prepare one sheet for each item on

Questionnaire #2. As responses come in, the comments could be recorded on that sheet as follows:

> ITEM #1: The car wash is never open when the client has time to use it.

> RANKINGS: (from the vote tally sheet) 7+4+5+2+1+1+7 +3+4+1+1+1 = 37

COMMENTS:

"Sunday afternoon is the only time I can really get my car washed in daylight. We get out of church at noon and that's when both our town car washes close."

"My car sits in our parking lot at work, along with three thousand other cars, from 7:30 A.M. until 4:30 P.M. I seem to always make it to the car wash just as it closes."

"I don't see that this is an important issue at all. It's just a question of priorities. If I really want my car washed, I could arrange my schedule to meet theirs. What gripes me is the idea of rearranging my schedule so I can pay those robbers $2.75 to do a (censored) poor job on my car."

"It seems to me this is just another example of how today's capitalists are so busy earning money that they never think of the little people. If they really want my business, they'll find some way to bring the car wash to me or my car to the car wash and do it in a way that doesn't inconvenience me."

The work group might summarize the items in one of the two ways mentioned. In the first method, duplications would be eliminated and the items presented as follows:

> "Car washes close during clients' free time, such as Sunday afternoons, before and after work."

> "There are points such as factory parking lots where many potential clients store their cars."

> "Hours are not seen to be as critical as cost and quality."

> "Are there ways in which a car could be washed without the client's having to deliver it to the car wash?"

As an alternative, a paragraph summarization might be as follows:

"Respondents generally felt that hours were a problem though possibly not as great as cost and quality. Some respondents felt that more creative means of access were needed that minimized client involvement."

Now the work group must decide if the respondent panel is providing the hoped-for information. At this point it is not too late to change the questionnaire if the responses aren't useful. For example, if it becomes clear that the comments and items received are too specific, Questionnaire #3 can reclassify items under headings that are much broader.

The following questions can help the work group determine the value of Questionnaire #2:

"Suppose that the items, votes, and comments on Questionnaire #2 were the final step of your Delphi. What decisions would you make and why? What is valuable or troublesome about responses so far?"

If the work group isn't obtaining the responses that it needs to make decisions, it should change the direction of the Delphi study. This is accomplished by making questions either more general or more specific. Remember, data collection for data's sake is worthless. If the responses won't help decision makers, then the question format of the Delphi study must be changed.

8) Develop Questionnaire #3 and test

The original purpose of our Delphi study was to generate consensus on issues of importance. Toward that end, issues have been identified (Questionnaire #1), clarifications, supportive statements, and criticisms made (Questionnaire #2), and a preliminary indication of priorities obtained through rankings. This third and final questionnaire permits the participants to review prior responses and express their individual judgments as to the importance of each item.[5]

5. The number of Delphi questionnaires may vary from three to five, depending on the degree of agreement and amount of additional information being sought or obtained. For illustrative purposes, we have arbitrarily chosen a three-questionnaire Delphi.

The benefits are as follows:

1) It provides closure for the study.
2) It suggests areas where diversity of judgment exists, but allows for the aggregation of judgments.
3) It provides guidelines for future research and planning.

Some additional words about these benefits will be helpful.

Closure: Participants like to feel that their effort was worthwhile. This final questionnaire provides closure by permitting respondents to vote on items developed in Questionnaire #1 and clarified in Questionnaire #2.

Diversity of judgment: Priorities can be aggregated by voting, but individual differences in judgment may still exist. The magnitude of these differences and characteristics of respondents whose opinions differ are important information to know as a guide to further program planning. For example, if a sizable minority view an item as important, this information is just as important a planning clue as the identification of agreed-upon priorities. The final questionnaire permits us to measure both diversity and agreement.

Guidelines for future research and planning: The results of the Delphi study provide guidance to program planners. If the Delphi was used to identify problems, the priority rankings suggest early issues to address in solution programs. If the Delphi was used to identify essential components of a solution, priority rankings suggest which components are important features in the new program. Delphi was used to identify factors to be considered in program evaluation; the outcome suggests the weight to be given to each factor in an evaluation design.

Mechanics • The mechanics of the third questionnaire parallel earlier efforts. A letter, a self-addressed, stamped envelope, and a questionnaire should be sent to respondents. An illustration of the format for Questionnaire #3, using the car-wash illustration, is given in Figure 4–6.

The questionnaire format should make it easy for respondents to identify the final items to which reactions are being sought, the results from the earlier vote, and the differences of opinion about their value. It should encourage further comments and elicit a vote. As with the other questionnaires, it should require thirty minutes to complete and should be pilot-tested before being sent out.

FIGURE 4–6.

		QUESTIONNAIRE #3	
FINAL VOTE REQUESTED	PRELIM-INARY VOTE RESULTS	ITEM	SUMMARY OF EARLIER COMMENTS
_____	63 _____	1) The car wash is *not* *open* when the client has time to use it (hours)	Respondents generally felt that hours were a problem though possibly not as great as cost and quality. Some respondents felt that more creative means of access were needed that minimized client involvement.
		etc.	

9) *Analysis of Questionnaire #3*

The analysis of Questionnaire #3 follows the same procedure as the analysis of Questionnaire #2. Particular care should be taken to ensure clarity in preparation of this final statement of results so that individuals who did not participate in the Delphi study understand the summary categories and phrasing.

10) *Prepare a final report*

Participants and work group members have put a lot of work into the Delphi study. Both deserve feedback. The analysis of Questionnaire #3 can be used as a partial vehicle for that feedback. However, a final report should summarize the goals and the process as well as the results. The final report may also lend legitimacy to actions taken by decision makers. That is, if a Delphi is used in development of a conference agenda, it is important to write a brief report to show how the Delphi influenced the conference itself. If a Delphi is used to make decisions regarding policy, it should be possible to return a position paper that was developed on the basis of Questionnaire #3. In any case, it is essential that the participants be given a summary of the results from Questionnaire #3 in order to achieve closure to the Delphi process.

MODIFICATIONS TO DELPHI

The above is not the only Delphi format. Delphi is a decision-making tool and should be modified to respond to the needs of the individual decision makers. Some examples of modifications are given below.

Some Delphi studies have used cassette tapes as a response mode rather than questionnaires. Respondents seem to react favorably. In most cases it is easier to talk about a subject than to write about it. However, it should be remembered that the analysis time is greatly increased because each tape has to be listened to, transcribed, and analyzed.

Some Delphi studies stop after the second questionnaire. If a final vote is not needed and clarification is not important, it may be sufficient to feed back to respondents the analysis of the second Delphi questionnaire.

Some Delphi studies start with a questionnaire similar to our Questionnaire #2. That is, the work group might use a technique such as NGT to identify items, then use the Delphi Technique to obtain wider participation in responding and voting.

Other Delphi studies ask for comments on the second questionnaire only from people who appear to be out of line with the majority consensus. For instance, if a respondent ranks highly an item that no one else selects, he or she is asked to defend that position. However, such a process can appear to be coercion, resulting in regression toward the mean.

We have included as an appendix portions of a four-questionnaire Delphi used by the School of Nursing at the University of Wisconsin to structure a conference on nursing role realignment. We appreciate their willingness to let us include this illustration.

REFERENCES

Dalkey, Norman C. *Delphi*. Rand Corporation, 1967.
Helmer, Olaf. *Analysis of the Future: The Delphi Method*. Rand Corporation, 1967.

Kaufman, Jerome, and David H. Gustafson. *Multi-County Land Use Policy Formation: A Delphi Analysis.* Technical Report of the Department of Industrial Engineering, University of Wisconsin, Madison, 1973.

Pyke, Donald, and Harper North. "Technological Forecasting to Aid Research and Development Planning." *Research Management,* XII, 4 (1969).

Turoff, Murray. "Delphi and Its Potential Impact on Information Systems." *AFIPS Conference Proceedings,* 39 (1971): 317–26.

Wisconsin Governor's Health Task Force. "Wisconsin Health Delivery Research and Development System." *Research and Information Supplement,* II (November 1973).

Applying NGT in Planning Situations

5

NGT and the Delphi Technique can be utilized *within* organizations to facilitate problem solving between managers and staff. However, they are also powerful techniques for bringing together *outside* resources, for such tasks as exploratory research and the structuring of participation in developmental planning endeavors. Indeed, NGT was originally conceived as a participation technique for social-planning situations. Although this chapter will focus upon applications of NGT, Chapter 4 has suggested how the same principles can be applied utilizing a Delphi approach.

We will take up the following application areas of frequent concern to developmental planners:

      Exploratory research
      Citizen participation
      Utilization of multidisciplinary experts
      Proposal review

EXPLORATORY RESEARCH [1]

The term "research," even when applied to developmental planning, often suggests the following situation:

1) The problem is clearly defined and the task is merely to obtain detailed elaborating or supporting information.
2) The essential causal relationships are known and agreed upon.
3) Critical variables and interrelationships can be quantitatively reduced and manipulated.

The world of planners engaged in exploratory or pilot research is, however, quite different. A number of critical differences are immediately apparent:

1) The involvement of consumers often means that attitudinal, emotional, and interpersonal variables may be important research concerns.
2) Little clinical, let alone analytical, understanding of some variables may exist.
3) Language barriers exist between professionals, administrators, and laymen, all of whom are important reference groups.
4) Multiple professional disciplines are often involved so that analytic models within a particular discipline may not be easily communicated across disciplines.
5) Political variables and vested interests of institutions may become important.
6) Qualitative political and emotional concerns may not be easily subjected to quantitative reduction and manipulation.

By definition, then, *exploratory* or *pilot research* is concerned with the investigation of complex problems whose qualitative and quantitative parameters are unknown.

1. *This discussion draws from Delbecq and Van de Ven, 1972.*

Measurement in planning

NGT has often been used as a pilot research technique prior to the use of more traditional measurement techniques[2] such as questionnaires and field interviews. In other instances, however, NGT itself is sufficient to generate the informed judgments and rough, qualitative data required to proceed into subsequent phases of planning.

The quality of a planner's research effort will be judged, in part, by the appropriateness of the data collection techniques employed. The purpose of any measurement procedure is to produce *reliable* information which is *valid* and relevant to the questions being asked by the planner and the decisions to be made (Jahoda, Deutsch, and Cook, 1951). A measurement procedure is considered reliable when repeated measurements using the same technique yield dependable, consistent, or stable data (Guilford, 1954; Nunnally, 1968). A measurement procedure is valid when it measures what it is intended to measure (Nunnally, 1968); i.e., the procedure produces relevant information about the object under investigation (Jahoda et al., 1951). However, achieving this purpose is difficult in exploratory research, for all the reasons suggested above. Because of this, the use of standard research instruments, particularly the mailed questionnaire and the interview, may be inappropriate (Heller, 1969).

For example, consider the measurement difficulties confronting a health planner who is faced with the problem of exploring the health-care needs of disadvantaged citizens in a particular geographical area and developing a program to respond to those needs.

In order to secure relevant data, the planner must know what questions to investigate. However, the development of questions for mailed questionnaires or field interviews presupposes that the planner conducting the research has clearly formulated the critical dimensions of the problem and knows what kinds of questions will elicit the data needed for analysis of the health-care program under investigation. In addition, knowing what language or stimulus clues will elicit responses from different reference groups (e.g., consumers, administrators, professionals, and technicians) is critical (Jahoda et al., 1951; Merton and Kendall, 1946). Thus, before quantifiable research measures can be

---

2. *In this section the terms "data collection techniques," "research instruments," "measurement procedures," and "measurement techniques" will be used synonymously.*

developed for data collection, the planner must have a qualitative understanding of the major parameters of the problem, as perceived by the
various reference groups, and a knowledge of reference group jargon;
otherwise, the collected data may be invalid.

Developing a qualitative understanding

Many planning situations require data input from such multiple
reference or *target* groups. The problem, however, is not simply language. Along with its own language structure, each group also has its
own perspective concerning the major parameters of the problem under
investigation.

Therefore, in much exploratory research a period of pilot exploration may be needed to develop an adequate qualitative understanding of the problem area and to acquaint planners with the
language useful in eliciting information from varied groups—this is
necessary before constructing other data collection instruments which
produce quantitative data. In addition, a clear understanding of the
qualitative dimensions of the problem area inevitably implies that the
target groups most closely associated with the problem must inform
the researcher of the critical issues endemic to the problem (Merton
and Kendall, 1946).

Let us return to our example, in terms of a consumer reference
group. It is not enough for the health researcher to learn that disadvantaged citizens regard hospital services in the geographical area
as "satisfactory," "dehumanizing," or "unacceptable." These judgments
are consistent with a variety of interpretations. For a researcher to
understand the citizens' perceived qualitative dimensions of hospital
services, a process is needed wherein the citizens can clarify what
"satisfactory," etc., denotes to them in this context: what were the
critical incidents or experiences which gave rise to these feelings; what
specific hospital services came to mind; are these issues perceived by
one individual or many; etc.

Finally, a process is needed whereby target groups can relate
critical incidents without feeling threatened. Otherwise, they may con-
ceal the actual character of their experiences. In some instances, a
target group's interview responses are distorted to accommodate the
reactions of the interviewer and the structure of the interview schedule.
As a result, items of concern may be underemphasized or excluded.

NGT as a pilot research technique

NGT is a useful technique to deal with many of the problems just listed as characteristic of exploratory research. NGT can be used to:

1) Identify and enrich the researcher's understanding of a problem by providing judgmental item identification, refined by priority ranking and voting.

2) Arrive at a set of hypotheses concerning the meaning and effects of determinate aspects of the problem area.

3) Focus attention on the major areas of inquiry, defined by target groups in their own jargon, which may be pursued in greater detail later by means of interview or questionnaire instruments.

In addition, NGT can be used to qualitatively explore either objective organizational or environmental problems or, alternatively, the affectional (emotional and expressive) dimensions of a problem (Van de Ven and Delbecq, 1971).

Prior to an NGT meeting, the planner selects samples of individuals (target groups) whose experience, expertise, or perceptions directly relate to the problem area being explored. For example, if the planner's objective is to identify the health-care problems experienced by citizens in a geographical area, the consumer target group might include a cross-section of residents divided according to age or other stratified criteria.

Each target group is brought together (either in a large meeting room or at several separate locations) and divided into small groups of individuals for the NGT meetings. The structured procedure described in Chapter 3 is followed by each individual group of eight participants.

Methodological difficulties

Three methodological difficulties are often encountered by researchers in utilizing NGT for exploratory research:

1) The selection of target groups for problem exploration.

2) The specification of the question to be used in NGT meetings for gathering data from target groups.

3) The transformation of this raw data into standardized measurement instruments.

These methodological difficulties will be discussed in turn, followed by a summary of the potential advantages of NGT as an exploratory research instrument.

Selection of target groups • Research suggests that a valid assessment of a problem area can be accomplished by the involvement of different target groups. This research substantiates the differences in perspectives on a problem area that exist between different target groups (Flanagan, 1954; Hoffman, 1965; Hoffman and Maier, 1961; Hoffman and Smith, 1960; Wagner, 1950). For example Smet (1952) carried out a study with faculty and students to determine the critical requirements for instructors of general psychology courses. As might be expected, significant differences emerged between the patterns of requirements listed by students and those listed by faculty. Thus, these studies indicate that in order to gain a comprehensive understanding of a problem under investigation, several NGT sessions should be conducted, using target groups whose experience directly relates to the problem area, but from different perspectives.

In the course of conducting NGT sessions with different target groups, the planner will want to generate information relating to their particular sphere of insight. Thus, for example, an NGT question in a meeting with consumers of hospital services might request participants to relate critical incidents (Flanagan, 1954), anticipated problems or fears (Delbecq and Van de Ven, 1971), or difficulties they experienced obtaining health-care services in a hospital. The most important problem dimensions identified in such a meeting could then be used as the input for an NGT session with the providers of health care. The NGT task statement with providers might be to "diagnose the critical components of the problem dimensions defined in the session with consumers" (Flanagan, 1954), or, "list alternative solution components to the priority problem dimensions" (Delbecq and Van de Ven, 1971).

From the foregoing discussion, it is clear that NGT is essentially a process for generating qualitative insight regarding critical problem dimensions. It should be emphasized that for a comprehensive assessment of the problem area to emerge: (1) several NGT sessions are needed with different target groups; (2) information must be requested from each target group in terms of their unique area of insight; and (3) the wording of the question in the NGT task statement must be properly focused and easily understood. The next section will explore this last issue of specifying the appropriate question.

Specification of the question • If the planner has sufficiently delineated the focus of the exploratory research problem, knows the relevant target groups to involve in a pilot study, and knows the information desired from each target group, then his attention can turn to question construction. This is the most crucial aspect of a data collection procedure (Flanagan, 1954).

Problems with the construction of research questions are well documented. Many studies have shown that a slight change in the wording of a question may produce substantial change in the character of the data generated (e.g., Muscio, 1916; Payne, 1951; Speak, 1967). In addition, there are subtle biases involved in the grammatical structure of the question which are not immediately apparent.

In most cases, the question should develop directly from the specific objectives of the NGT meeting. As an aid to developing the NGT question, the following question should be kept in mind: "What insightful or crucial information does each target group possess that would help us understand the dimensions of the problem?" Alternative NGT task statements should then be formulated and pilot-tested with a small sample of individuals from each target group, as discussed in Chapter 3.

Even after the pilot test of a question, there may still be problems regarding the interpretations of questions by respondents (Crutchfield and Gordon, 1947; Heller, 1969; Weitz, 1950; Wells, 1963). People interpret the same question according to widely different frames of reference (Campbell, 1945; Dean, 1958). The average person's knowledge of commonly used words varies and, therefore, responses to questions differ (Thorndike and Gallup, 1944).

As a general rule, in an NGT meeting with a target group we favor a broad question which elicits varied responses. These responses, evaluated by rating and ranking, can provide a researcher's first step in determining critical problem dimensions. Later, as a prelude to scaled survey or interview questions, further meetings can focus on refined issues. Broader questions can also provide clues for later research as to a group's jargon, since the group has to express the problem dimension in their own words. Thus, the NGT process may have to be repeated twice, moving from general to specific questions.

Content analysis of data • Of course, the raw data obtained in exploratory research by means of NGT does not automatically become useful in developing questionnaires or interview schedules. A necessary intermediate task is a content analysis of priority items.

A principal consideration in analyzing and classifying the data is its intended use. For example, if a major objective is to develop a set of hypotheses concerning the major dimensions of the problem and identification of specific areas of inquiry for standardized data collection instruments (such as questionnaires), then an appropriate classification system may be a set of priority headings or traits that eventually can be measured by means of scales. Three rules can guide the researcher in choosing measurable items from among the priority items:

1) Search for items that are observable in a variety of situations.

2) Search for items that seem to explain a large number of related phenomena.

3) Search for items that are easiest to measure and lowest in measurement cost (Hage, 1971).

According to Flanagan (1954), "The induction of categories from the raw item statements generated by NGT groups is a task which requires insight, experience, and objective judgment." Unfortunately, this procedure is more subjective than objective. However, Flanagan does offer a basic process for the content analysis of such data.

Begin by sorting a relatively small sample of items into piles according to the selected decision rules above. After these tentative categories are developed and approximately defined, classify additional items into them. Throughout this process, redefinitions of categories and the development of new categories occur frequently. The tentative categories are modified as needed, and the process is continued until all items are classified. The next step in the process is to determine the appropriate level of specificity for the categories. This involves consideration of the trade-off benefits of operational and specific categories as compared to the simplicity of a relatively small number of more generic categories (which may be more difficult to measure). For example, a generic category such as "poor communication" might be judged against the value of a specific category such as "insufficient market information; insufficient financial data."

The classification bias which necessarily enters the content analysis of the items can be reduced if a research *group* participates in the categorization process as opposed to one or two single researchers. In addition, a tentative categorization of the items could be submitted to experienced researchers and health-care professionals, as well as selected members of the target group who participated in NGT meetings, for review and modification.

Summary

Many research endeavors confronting planners are exploratory in nature. The development of viable and refined research instruments presupposes that the researcher has specified the critical dimensions of the problem under investigation, and has determined the exact language which should be used in questions and scales needed for refined quantitative analysis. Therefore, for many planning concerns, an exploratory research phase is needed to develop an adequate understanding of the problem area prior to research utilizing standard data collection techniques such as surveys or interviews.

To obtain a clinical understanding of the critical dimensions of the problem, the researcher must involve appropriate target groups in problem identification and interpretation. The successful identification of problem dimensions by target groups requires a research procedure that effectively generates a high quantity, quality, and variety of ideas, as well as identifies priority items. Based on these criteria, NGT is a powerful exploratory research technique. It allows multiple target groups to participate in defining problem dimensions, ranking and rating items generated, and expressing these items in their own jargon.

In conclusion, the potential usefulness of NGT as an exploratory research technique can be summarized. NGT:

1) Allows target groups to single out critical problem dimensions, by means of a process which is unthreatening and depersonalized.

2) Through discussion, clarifies the meaning of critical items for both researchers and participants.

3) Can be used to explore both the objective and subjective (emotional) dimensions of a problem.

4) Identifies priority concerns by means of voting procedures.

5) Facilitates the development of hypotheses and the formulation of questions for survey and interview field research.

6) Can be implemented in a short time period for several different target groups at low cost.

7) Includes a sufficient sample size to provide useful guidelines for more traditional data-gathering technologies.

This section has attempted to explain the potential benefits of NGT as an exploratory research instrument. As with other research instruments, it is designed for a special purpose. For some exploratory research problems, NGT is appropriate; for others it is not. In the final analysis, the prudent researcher will take heed in looking for the combination of methods best adapted to the specific task at hand.

CITIZEN PARTICIPATION

There is probably no more controversial topic than the relative merits versus problems of involving citizens or consumers in the planning process. Volumes have been written on the topic. However, even though great efforts have been made to include citizens, successes have been more limited. Citizens often feel that attempts to involve them have been window-dressing. In critical meetings they often feel that articulate professionals have greater influence due to verbal skills, and that consumer inputs are taken less seriously due to the consumer's lower status. Professionals, on the other hand, report that sincere efforts to involve citizens have not produced results equal to the costs. They complain that citizen inputs are more often rhetorical than substantive, that the stylistic manners of citizens are disruptive, and that citizens lack sufficient "expertise" to make viable contributions.

Why involve citizens?

There seem to be two major rationales for the involvement of citizens in developmental planning. The first relates to political philosophy, and the second to studies of innovation.

In terms of political philosophy, a major defense of citizen participation is based on the position of *subsidiarity*, that is, that governmental decisions should be decentralized as close to local or regional problems as possible. Citizen participation in this framework is concerned with making planning more responsive to the citizen by increasing his representation in the planning process, thus making planning priorities more responsive to citizen needs.

In terms of studies on innovation, the thrust of contemporary research on this topic suggests that organizations making major innovations have a heightened awareness of consumer needs. As a result they design their products or services in light of the concerns of the potential user (Science Policy Research Unit, 1972). Thus, successful organizations engage in market research, which aids the firms in producing and marketing products tailored to the preferences of the consumer. This is not, however, simply catering to "uneducated" consumer whims. Rather, this process allows organizations to design features into products or services which are easily overlooked by engineers but which are important to the consumer. In service organizations, this means designing programs which incorporate features to attend to unmet needs in order to obtain greater user satisfaction. Successful planners, therefore, will not ask for resource allocations unless they can provide unmanipulated evidence of unmet consumer needs.

Finally, the literature on innovation suggests that successful change must be preceded by a heightened awareness and tension concerning unmet needs or unsolved problems; otherwise, resources will not be allocated to design and implement new programs. Citizen involvement in this context seeks to portray in visible terms the unmet needs to which the planner is seeking to respond in order to obtain new resources or resource reallocations (Dalton, 1969). In this sense, the evidence of unmet needs allows consumers to act as a driving force in obtaining resources.

Problem identification
versus priority setting

In order to show that NGT is a useful tool for citizen participation, we need to suggest that there are two different dimensions to the issue. Much of the literature on innovation confuses: (1) the involvement of final users of products or services in defining unmet needs or inadequacies of present products or services; and (2) the relative influence of citizens or consumers in setting priorities. Although consumers should have a role in both concerns, their most unique and influential role should be identification of needs. However, the process by which consumers identify needs is often poorly structured.

For example, in order to increase awareness of student needs, universities are increasingly placing students on faculty and institutional planning committees. In like manner ethnic minorities are often placed on public planning boards. These few representatives are then expected to "speak for" the community, the student body, etc., in need identification. Such a position is obviously fraught with difficulties:

> Is the representative really *"representative"* of the average member of the group he or she purports to represent?
>
> Can the representative adequately *articulate* the position of the group he or she purports to represent?
>
> Is the verbal skill of the representative sufficient to *convince* the policy body of the realities which need to be communicated?
>
> Does the representative become more like the members of the policy body and cease to *perceive* problems like members of the group he or she represents over the term of service on the policy body?
>
> Will the representative become *co-opted* in his or her desire to ascend to increasing professional or community power?
>
> Does the representative really *communicate back* to the reference group or does he or she speak in an editorial "we" merely pretending to be informed?
>
> If he or she is informed, who are the informers? An average cross-section or a *militant* minority group?

The list could go on. Further, our research suggests that these are not specious problems (Delbecq, Van de Ven, and Wallace, 1972). Citizen participation or consumer involvement, then, cannot be restricted to seating representatives on a policy board, whatever the proportional representation might be. It must also involve some process analogous to market research, such as NGT. Accurate information about a cross-section of consumers is important to both professionals and consumers on a policy board. For the professional, it provides assurance that the statements of consumer representatives do indeed reflect real needs and widely shared perceptions. For the consumer representative, research on consumer needs forms the basis for taking a strong policy position, building coalitions with other members of the policy board, and bringing the weight of public opinion and the media to bear on a recalcitrant board. For all of the above reasons, distributive information must be coupled with representation on policy boards if citizen or consumer participation is to lead to maximum organizational understanding of unmet or partially met needs rather than "maximum feasible misunderstanding."

NGT as a mechanism
for consumer involvement

The advantages of NGT as a pilot research instrument, set forth earlier in the chapter, are equally applicable here. NGT allows consumer groups to identify critical problem dimensions in a manner which is unthreatening and depersonalized. This is particularly important in dealing with disadvantaged consumers. Because the process allows items to be generated and recorded in the jargon of the consumer, citizens are less threatened than by "professionally led" discussions, interviews, or surveys. The one critical modification to the NGT process is that the recorder may have to help disadvantaged citizens reduce their input to a brief phrase in Step 2 (round-robin listing). It is important, therefore, that recorders be from the same ethnic or minority background as consumers, so that recorders both understand the nuances of the input and use language in listing items that is consistent with the jargon of the group members.

NGT likewise can help the research group clarify the meaning of the problems listed and explore objective and subjective dimensions of the problems. Also, the process can be implemented in a short time period with a sufficient sample to yield indicative results which can later be substantiated by survey research.

Special advantages of NGT

NGT, however, has some special advantages in this particular application; that is, it:

1) Helps justify the need for more thorough research into citizen needs and perceptions.

2) Reduces some destructive interaction dynamics characteristic of nonprofessionals.

3) Reduces some of the disadvantages of mixing citizens with professionals.

4) Ensures that important citizen needs are adequately presented to policy bodies.

5) Provides a basis on which citizen representatives can attempt to influence policy bodies.

6) Places professionals in a reactive position in the planning process, if citizen input is the first phase of planning.

One characteristic of professionals is that they feel confident of their knowledge base. In our experience, professionals are always sure they "know" what the problems of consumers are. However, in every instance when we have asked consumers to indicate their priority concerns, there has been a significant difference in the concerns identified by them as compared to the concerns listed by professionals. It is not so much that the professionals are wrong, but rather that their list of concerns is incomplete since they perceive problems from a different perspective than do consumers. This reality places citizen representatives in a difficult position. Either they must become aggressive "advocates," in which case the professionals soon feel they are unduly abrasive, or they must selectively present demands, which means that many consumer concerns are neglected. NGT allows citizen representatives to replace arguments with indicative exploratory *data* obtained from NGT meetings. For example, student representatives involved in a curriculum committee at a university can use NGT results to identify student concerns about courses under consideration. It is almost axiomatic to say that students will be concerned with some matters that are not perceived by or are of low interest to faculty. Rather than arguing with faculty representatives, the student representative can simply present the results of NGT meetings conducted with a sample of students. Such a step might: legitimate inclusion of student concerns in curriculum planning, which might otherwise be ignored; justify further research of student curriculum concerns of a more refined nature; and reorganize allocation of committee priorities in the design of the new curriculum.

NGT has the additional advantage of avoiding destructive interaction both within the NGT meeting, and between consumers and professionals. Consumer groups often do not have the analytical discipline or training to focus on problem-centered material, avoid unnecessary anecdotal and personal information, and reach a final decision in an orderly manner. The NGT meeting provides structured mechanisms which allow groups of individuals with limited skills to generate, clarify, and evaluate concerns.

Militant representatives of citizens or consumers often confront professionals with rhetoric which alienates the latter. As Lipsky has pointed out, in order to appear charismatic, militant citizen leaders are often prone to substitute rhetorical and psychological rewards for more refined analysis. As a result, these militant representatives often master the art of overstatement, which might please constituents, but which interferes with problem solving (Lipsky, 1971). A proper NGT question can focus the attention of consumer groups on a less emotional level, thus helping to avoid psychological and ideological statements by self-appointed leaders. Our own experience has been that rhetorical leaders are not able to dominate problem-centered discussion by citizens or consumers in NGT meetings.

Thus, after refinement by staff, NGT output from meetings with citizens is often more acceptable to professionals than direct interaction with citizens. The same consumer concerns, when translated into more refined language and communicated as NGT output, may elicit more sympathetic responses than a direct, personal confrontation between a panel of citizens and professionals.

NGT allows broader sampling as well. The planning group may tap several different groups of consumers so that it does not focus its response on a particular group which claims to be representative of all consumers. An obvious advantage of the relatively simple and low-cost aspect of NGT is that a sample of thirty-five individuals from five reference groups can often be tapped at less than the cost of interviewing a smaller sample of a single reference group.

The summary of critical problem dimensions, phrased in comfortable terms for professionals and resource controllers, represents the output of NGT meetings with consumers. This output is also the basis on which consumer representatives can lobby to see that legitimate concerns of consumers are not neglected in the planning process, even if these concerns differ from the priorities of professionals. If indeed professionals remain insensitive, then this output or data can be the basis for political or media pressures on a policy board.

Finally, there is the matter of beginning a planning process with professional input versus beginning with citizen input. The more traditional sequence has been for professionals to focus on their own concerns in planning and designing, and *then* ask for citizen input in the form of reactions to their recommended solutions. At this point it is difficult to accommodate neglected consumer concerns, since acknowledgement of deficiencies in the professionals' plan seems to directly question its adequacy.

By contrast, by obtaining citizen input as a prior step to professional design, the creative abilities of professionals to design plans, programs, or services which encompass consumer as well as professional concerns is tapped. Thus, we strongly favor a planning process which begins with consumer or citizen need identification (Delbecq and Van de Ven, 1971). The NGT process allows the planner to assess the nature and degree of consumer concerns inexpensively, and to assess the extent to which further citizen participation in problem identification is desirable.

Summary

The NGT process is a helpful tool for obtaining citizen or consumer input prior to solution exploration and the design of new products, programs, or services. As such, it has been widely adopted as one type of citizen or consumer participation in planning. Such research-oriented participation is obviously not a substitute for citizen representation on planning and policy boards. However, without NGT as a complementary process, much of this representation is weak, ineffectual, misleading, and conducive to misunderstanding. We will return to the issue of citizen participation as it relates to representation on policy, planning, and review boards when we take up the questions of proposal review and priority setting later in this chapter.

Much of the disillusionment with citizen or consumer participation has been generated by expecting laymen to be equal to professionals in the *design* of solutions to problems. This is obviously a specious expectation. The unique and special role of laymen in planning, in our view, is to ensure that consumer needs are understood, and that proposed solutions are tested in terms of the extent to which consumer needs are met. This would imply that laymen are most central in the problem exploration and proposal review phases of planning. The fact that they are less central (although often helpful) in design phases of planning is hardly reason to feel that their involvement is unwarranted. Problem identification and evaluation of proposals, after all, are equally important aspects of planning as solution exploration and design. Finally, consumer involvement in the total process is an important aspect of building the basis for later adoptions of pilot programs by other organizations. The total burden of evidence favors increasing the effectiveness of such involvement rather than allowing past failures and insufficient skill in structuring participation to justify regressing to professional dominance of planning endeavors.

UTILIZATION OF MULTIDISCIPLINARY
EXPERTS

A critical task for all planners involved in developmental endeavors is to *identify* knowledge resources and to *involve* multidisciplinary and multi-agency experts in the design of innovative solutions.
The need to do so reflects both the "information explosion" and the
specialization of knowledge which is characteristic of present-day society.
Information in scientific fields is doubling every six to ten years. To
cope with this information explosion, professional and scientific personnel have become increasingly specialized. Thus, it is unlikely that
any single discipline can provide all the answers to a problem.

Further, with the diffusion of high-quality personnel across
many organizations, universities, etc. (partially the result of increased
graduate education across the nation), identifying resource experts
often involves a movement outside of one's own organization, and even
outside one's own geographic region, even if the organization itself is
elite and the metropolitan area large. No single university, agency, or
urban area, no matter how renowned, will have a monopoly on quality
resource people whose insights could contribute to innovative solutions.

Although the above statements have been popularized into conventional truisms in best sellers such as *Future Shock* (Toffler, 1970),
studies of the behavior of planners and scientists show there are powerful dynamics which still limit most searches for solutions. It is typical
for the leader of a group to invite individuals with whom he or she
is already acquainted to serve as the exclusive resource panel in exploring solutions to a developmental planning problem. Indeed, the
most powerful predictors of who will be invited to any meeting are:
(1) individuals who are physically proximate to the person calling
the meeting; and (2) individuals with whom the person calling the
meeting has shared other task activities (Delbecq, 1972).

Therefore, planners need a conscious strategy to *identify*
diverse sources of knowledge, and to *involve* these sources of knowledge in exploring solutions to complex problems. NGT can be a useful
device for both purposes. It can discipline planners to reach outside
their normal network of acquaintances so as to involve outside resource people, and it can facilitate the creative involvement of these
people in specifying components of a creative solution.

Normally, finding an innovative solution to a complex problem
in developmental planning involves two distinct phases which require
separate meetings. The first is *knowledge exploration,* a search for

major conceptual frameworks and broad insights. The second is *solution exploration,* the refinement of broad insights by specifying components which should be included in the solution program. This often means that two different sets of resource persons are needed: (1) in the early phase, individuals capable of broad conceptualization and strategic thinking; and (2) at a later phase, technical experts who can identify the components to be included in the solution plan.

An NGT format
for knowledge exploration

Resource people are generally not free-floating, that is, they are normally part of some organization, institution, or activity group. Three broad categories should be kept in mind when searching for potential sources of outside experts: (1) disciplines or skills; (2) organizations; and (3) related literature. NGT has often been used to identify possible knowledge resources, with the following simple format serving as leadership guidelines for the meeting:

> 1) Present a visual display of critical problem elements identified by consumers, field workers, and professionals:
> > a. explain the exploratory research generating the problem elements.
> > b. clarify the meaning of the problem elements.
> 2) Present an NGT "Knowledge Resource Nomination Worksheet" with the following headings:
> > a. Disciplines or Skills
> > b. Organizations:
> > Research
> > Professional
> > Provider/Delivery
> > Funding
> > c. Related Literature
> 3) Have the group participate in an NGT process wherein the members generate a list of potential resource groups or organizations to contact under each of the above headings for knowledge exploration.

In summary, the leader carefully briefs the participants on the priority problem elements, and allows them to generate, list, discuss, and rank resource groups. As we will discuss later, the results of this process are eventually used to obtain nominations of specific individuals who might become active members of a solution exploration meeting.

At first glance, this process might seem somewhat elaborate. In fact, it is simply accomplished. We can illustrate the procedure by recounting a family incident.

One of the authors followed this process in identifying resource groups to help him design a doghouse for his bull mastiff, a 140-pound family pet. The dog had been purchased in the summer as a puppy, so that a doghouse did not become an issue until fall. At that time several problems were identified by the family as priority concerns to which a "doghouse" solution was to be found (Figure 5–1).

FIGURE 5–1.   Problem Element List.

The doghouse should be located and constructed so the dog has access to the entire yard for exercise.

The dog should not be so insulated from sights and sounds that he ceases to be an effective watchdog.

The doghouse should be located so the children can continue to feel the dog was their pet.

The doghouse should be constructed to provide healthy conditions in severe winter weather.

The doghouse should be built with the possibility of another companion dog being added to the family at a later time.

Normally, one would talk to a couple of co-workers and run off to construct the doghouse on a sunny weekend. Instead the family developed a Knowledge Resource Nomination Worksheet (Figure 5–2).

The family divided up the responsibility for contacting representatives from the disciplines and organizations and checking their literature list. As a result, at a later meeting, they specified critical solution components (Figure 5–3).

In Father's mind prior to the knowledge resource nomination step, the doghouse had been very large (which the dog could not have heated by body heat), uninsulated, and constructed of plywood

FIGURE 5-2.   Knowledge Resource Nomination Worksheet.

[Disciplines or Skills]	*[Organizations]*	*[Related Literature]*
1. Veterinarian	1. American Kennel Club	1. *Dog World* Magazine
2. Professional Breeder	(AKC)	2. AKC Encyclopedia
3. Builder	2. Local Kennel Club	3. Handyman's Encyclopedia
4. Architect	3. Agricultural Extension	4. Local Branch Library
	Service	
	4. Humane Society	
	5. American Bull Mastiff	
	Association	

(more subject to splintering, chewing, and moisture), with a burlap flap (decreasing light and air), located in the back of the yard (a muddy trail for the children to see Fido), facing the house (into the prevailing wind). While many dog fanciers would have known better, a doghouse was a challenging building endeavor to the amateur dog owner. The results of the NGT Knowledge Resource Nomination Worksheet motivated Father to enlarge the design discussion to include "outside experts" who identified critical components of a more innovative and successful solution. Obviously, this is a simple example of knowledge exploration. Much more important is the application of the same process to complex planning situations.[3]

Process guidelines • The following guidelines will facilitate the knowledge exploration process:

· Make the nominations of disciplinary skills *multidisciplinary*.
· Identify key organizations in different geographical regions.
· Avoid simply identifying individuals.

On the NGT Knowledge Resource Nomination Worksheet, *Disciplines or Skills* refers to theoretical, empirical, or technical skills which can be brought to bear on the problem(s) under study. This list should emphasize multidisciplinary skills. It is easy for a group to concentrate within their own discipline and thus reach too narrowly for resources.

In identifying organizations, several suggestions are helpful. First, staff should try to identify multiple geographic locations. For example, even universities and research centers tend to have regional identifications and limited national communication. Therefore, staff

3. *See Chapter 1 for a description of complex planning situations.*

FIGURE 5–3.   Solution Components and Source of Suggestion.

Basic Design:

A square doghouse, two times the volume of the dog, with an inner wall (so the dog can keep warm by body heat) [Veterinarian]

Hardboard floors (resist moisture, insects, and chewing) [Local Kennel Club]

Styrofoam insulation (retains less moisture) [Building Supplier]

Information concerning construction materials and building plan [Building Supplier]

An inner side installed between pegs so the house could be enlarged without redesign when a second dog was added [Building Supplier]

Inner wall instead of flap to allow for greater air movement during change of seasons [Professional Breeder]

Plastic window in inner wall to increase light and make the dog more willing to use during daylight hours in very cold weather [American Bull Mastiff Fanciers Newsletter]

Location:

Facing south (to avoid prevailing wind patterns) [AKC Encyclopedia]

On the edge of the patio (easy, nonmuddy access for children) [Architect Friend]

Within hearing of gate and yard entrance [Father]

Appearance:

Matching shingles on outside to blend with the house [Architect Friend]

Flower pots and shrubs around house to create gardenlike appearance [*House and Garden* Magazine]

Labor:

Father [having read basic building instructions in the handyman's encyclopedia]

should contact organizations in each of the four major regions: East, Midwest, South, and West. Second, in addition to organizations concerned with basic disciplines, staff should identify professional societies as well as producing, service, or provider organizations in one's own or related fields. Creativity is not merely a function of analysis (the role of scientific resources); it is also a function of sharing experiences (the role of professional or provider organizations). Finally, funding sources are often helpful nominators of organizations doing related work in the public sector. Foundations and federal agencies providing funding can often suggest both basic research and provider organizations whom they have funded for related projects.

One should also be sure that the group engaged in knowledge resource nomination does not simply identify individuals. While it is useful and helpful to have the names of specific persons, these contacts seldom represent the knowledge or activities of a field. Rather, they represent eclectic and chance contacts that reflect the personal associations of the nominator. The total list of knowledge resource nominations will have to be reduced to a manageable number of follow-up contacts in keeping with the personnel available and the complexity of the problem. This reduction is best accomplished by the usual NGT ranking procedure discussed in Chapter 3.

Finally, the composition of the group for NGT knowledge resource nomination is no less important than the composition for other purposes. It does not automatically follow that the regular staff is the sole proper NGT group membership for this exercise. Enlarging the group to include a *cosmopolitan* (someone with many contacts across organizations) from each of the basic reference groups greatly increases the creativity in nominations.

Follow-up to nominations

Acting upon the results of NGT knowledge resource nominations to determine who should be invited to a solution exploration meeting is a staff effort. Generally, follow-up is conducted by telephone. Pairs of individuals who were part of the NGT group are assigned the responsibility of telephone contact to obtain the names of specific *individuals* who are in the groups identified on the NGT worksheets. Individuals should not be asked to make contacts in organizations or fields with which they are not familiar or comfortable. For example, an individual from a provider agency far removed from university life preferably should not conduct the telephone contacts with academicians. (One of the reasons for expanding the composition of the NGT knowledge resource nomination group is to include a representative from each major reference category who might be willing to assist in follow-up.) Using pairs of individuals for telephone contact increases motivation and social support and decreases some of the burden of multiple phone calls. Each pair should totally cover a single discipline or professional area since this process is a talent hunt which builds on clues from one phone call to the next.

Figure 5–4 presents a work plan used by one organization for telephone contacts. It is a general guide which can be modified to fit the unique output of NGT knowledge resource nominations.

FIGURE 5–4.   A Work Guide for Telephone Follow-up of NGT Knowledge Resource Nominations.

Step One: Obtain Nominations of Individual Resource Persons

NGT knowledge resource nominations are nominations of groups (disciplines, provider organizations, etc.) rather than nominations of individuals. The first follow-up step, therefore, is designed to identify the names of individual resource persons. This is accomplished by a process of obtaining nominations of such resource persons from "cosmopolitans" or "boundary spanners." (The term cosmopolitan refers to individuals who have a wide range of contacts in their discipline, not restricted to their own organization. Another term sometimes used is "boundary spanner," that is, those who cross many boundaries within their field.)

The first step, then, is to contact cosmopolitans who can nominate specific resource persons whom you will later interview.

If you are dealing with a discipline with which you are familiar, cosmopolitans are easy to identify. However, in a strange field proxy variables must be used. For example, officers of professional associations or program chairmen of national associations should be contacted since a certain degree of eminence and communication centrality are usually a precondition for election to these positions. Likewise, department chairmen or people in key administrative positions are somewhat more likely to have contacts beyond their own organization, although this is a less reliable indicator than elective positions in regional or national organizations. One can increase the reliability of key administrators as nominators, however, by going to prestigious organizations since these organizations are often pivotal communication links. (For example, administrators in major graduate schools are more likely to have cosmopolitan contacts than administrators in small private or public colleges.)

The purpose of telephone contact is to obtain from the cosmopolitans nominations of resource persons who may have information about or be doing work in an area related to your problem category. In making these first phone calls to obtain nominations of resource persons, use the following process guidelines:

Process Guidelines

1. Determine if it is a convenient time to talk to the cosmopolitan. If not, return the call at a later time.
2. Explain your organizational affiliation.

FIGURE 5–4.   (Cont.)

3. Explain briefly the problem identification processes used in the exploratory research.
4. State clearly the priority problem(s) to which you are seeking solutions.
5. Ask the cosmopolitan if he or she can nominate specific resource individuals who might have information or experience which would help you.
6. Take notes concerning names, places to contact the individuals, and types of probable expertise.
7. Thank the nominator and follow up with a letter of thanks, which reviews the conversation and suggests that if other resource individuals come to mind the nominator should feel free to phone, collect.

Step Two: Contact the Individual Resource Persons Nominated

Process Guidelines

1. Determine if it is a convenient time to talk to the resource person. If not, return the call at a later time.
2. Explain your organizational affiliation.
3. Identify the nominator who suggested that you contact the resource person.
4. Give a brief overview of the problem(s) to which you are seeking solutions.
5. Ask the resource person to suggest:
   a. related literature (theory, research, working papers) [both the resource person's own work and the work of others]
   b. key ideas which come to mind
   c. nominations of other resource persons
6. Take notes concerning the resource person's:
   a. specific ideas and suggestions
   b. insight and special skills
   c. general interest
7. If you are favorably impressed with the resource person and feel he or she may have a substantial contribution to make to solution exploration, ask if the resource person would be willing to further explore the problem and potential solutions with a panel of other experts at a future date.
8. Express appreciation for assistance given.

A Final Word

It is important not to have false expectations concerning the results of such telephone contacts. Experience suggests that one fruitful telephone contact in six is a good results ratio. If one of the six calls leads to innovative solution components, the effort has been worthwhile.

Summary

In present-day society, the ability to involve outside resource persons is particularly important. More than half of the major innovations arrived at in the private sector incorporate major design features as a result of ideas obtained from external resources (Utterback, 1971). It is easy, however, to avoid the effort of contacting outsiders and much more typical to simply talk to one's own physically proximate colleagues.

The NGT knowledge resource nomination process discussed above stimulates a planning group to reach outside its own interaction network. Admittedly, it is easier to generate the list of potential information sources than to engage in telephone follow-up. Individual differences loom large in terms of the ability to successfully initiate contacts with organizational cosmopolitans, obtain nominations of resource individuals, make initial contact with these individuals, summarize key information, and determine who among the individuals contacted should be invited to a solution exploration meeting. Staff who do possess the necessary skills, however, often turn up important resources who greatly enhance the innovative scope of solution exploration. Such effort is warranted for a planning group studying potential solutions to complex developmental problems.

An NGT format
for solution exploration

Whether or not a planning group nominates and identifies resource persons according to a disciplined process such as that described above, eventually a group will meet to determine a solution program, based on available information and creative insight generated at a solution exploration meeting. For complex developmental planning, such a meeting must be preceded by identification of external experts whose disciplines or skills relate to the problems under consideration. Combined with internal organizational experts who are responsible for the drafting of a detailed proposal, this entire group of in-house and external knowledge resource people must jointly explore the critical features of an adequate solution program which later is reflected in the formal "proposal."

We would recommend the following leadership guidelines for structuring a solution exploration meeting utilizing an NGT format:

1) Visually display the critical problem elements identified in exploratory research for which a solution program is to be developed:

    a. clarify the meaning of the elements through discussion.

    b. answer remaining questions concerning the scope and character of the problem(s) and problem elements.

2) Define the role of the participants in the meeting (i.e., to serve as idea generators, not as theoreticians or organizational representatives).

3) Present NGT Solution Exploration Worksheets to the group (Figure 5-5) and explain the meaning of the response categories (i.e., *Solution Components, Existing Resources,* and *Potential Resources*).

4) Follow the NGT process of generating, listing, discussing, ranking, discussing vote, and reranking or rating of solution components.

Process guidelines • Some words about the process itself are in order before discussing the benefits of following such a structured approach.

Individuals coming to a solution exploration meeting often want to expostulate on their knowledge, not apply their knowledge to the problem to which a solution is being developed. Theoreticians

FIGURE 5-5.   Solution Exploration Worksheet.

[Solution Components]	[Existing Resources]	[Potential Resources]
1.		
2.		
3.		
4.		
5.		
6.		
7.		
8.		
9.		
10.		

would prefer to talk about their theory, and organizational representatives would prefer to tell the group how they are doing things in St. Louis. Therefore, a key concern is to focus the attention of the resource group on *your problem* and its key elements rather than on their back-home theoretical or experiential references. There are a number of steps which can be taken to accomplish this.

Visual display of the problem, detailed in terms of critical problem elements, is the first step. However, it is important that this visual display be reinforced and clarified by discussion.

Second, it is important to verbally define the role of participants as idea generators concerned with the creative development of a solution program which is *unique* to this problem setting. Thus, their role is to generate component parts of the solution from their theoretical and experiental frames of reference, rather than to explain other frameworks with which they are familiar. When asked to develop something new and unique people are generally flattered and therefore not offended about not being asked to provide theoretical models or tell "war stories."

Third, regarding the NGT Solution Exploration Worksheet itself, it is important to illustrate what is meant by a solution component, existing resource, and potential resource. Suppose the group is meeting to deal with a land use problem. In such an instance, an illustration from the field of education can be used to illustrate the point without "leading" the group. The leader could explain the response categories on the NGT worksheets as follows:

> "You will notice your worksheets have three categories: *Solution Components, Existing Resources,* and *Potential Resources.* Let me briefly explain what each category means.
>
> "*Solution components* are critical features which must be incorporated into a successful program to solve the problem(s) we have just outlined. For example, imagine we are meeting to plan an educational program for disadvantaged urban youngsters. Further, imagine that problem elements include: (1) a defeatist attitude; (2) unfamiliarity with the world of work; and (3) hostility toward institutions.
>
> "You would probably want to propose solution components for each problem element. For example, to deal with (2), unfamiliarity with the world of work, you might feel solution components should include: (a) introduction to career planning; (b) experience with major institutions through visitations;

and (c) prework experiences simulating work settings. *Existing resources* might include state employment services, junior achievement, or upward bound programs. *Potential resources* might include organizations or individuals presently thinking about or working on new or related activities."

The leader would then illustrate solution components, existing resources, and potential resources for a problem element actually a concern of the meeting underway, based on ideas obtained through telephone contact with a resource person not present.[4]

The remainder of the NGT process is sufficiently familiar to readers of Chapter 3 so as not to require further clarification except for one point. In rating and/or ranking, the vote relates only to the solution component category and not to the existing resources or potential resources categories. These latter two items on the worksheets are useful information for follow-up planning, and help illustrate additional resources for implementation. However, the more critical focus in the NGT solution exploration meeting is the emerging outline of a solution program and its component parts.

Special advantages of NGT

It is not necessary to enlarge on the advantages of this format relative to avoiding both "war stories" and rambling theoretical discussions which do not focus on the problem at hand. Planners are well aware that professionals are generally *not* more disciplined than laymen or citizens at large. Indeed, the richer information and more secure ego base of professionals allow them to talk at great length without great discipline. In this sense, this NGT format is equally as valuable in working with professional groups as the NGT problem exploration format is for working with citizen groups.

A second advantage is that, by asking for both existing re-

4. *Many of the resource persons contacted through NGT knowledge resource nominations will have neither ideas nor information other than that conveyed by telephone or available in writing. On the other hand, some resource persons will be deeply involved with concerns on which staff is seeking assistance. Staff will invite the latter resource persons to participate in the solution exploration meeting. However, staff will need to remember to share not only their own thinking about the problem, but also the important clues obtained through telephone contact and literature from other resource persons not present at the solution exploration meeting.*

sources and potential resources, NGT focuses the group's attention on the potential for pooling solution resources. It is aimed at avoiding unnecessary duplication of resources and encouraging collaborative programs across organizations.

A third advantage of the format is that the generation of eclectic solution components allows the group to explore a creative new (re)combination of solution concerns, rather than simply to modify an existing theoretical or experiential solution model. Research indicates that a critical element in achieving truly innovative solutions is encouraging individuals to search outside the framework of their previous experiences (Dalton, 1969).

The use of external resource persons from multiple disciplines and provider organizations, together with internal staff, also greatly increases the potential for developing a solution program composed of new or uniquely combined elements. In this respect, juxtaposing purely scientific personal with applied organizational specialists is particularly important. Research indicates that there are two types of creativity. One is concerned with *analysis,* identifying critical causal elements or dimensions. Another deals with *synthesis,* the ability to combine such elements into appropriate and feasible solution patterns (Gordan and Morse, 1968). The use of both disciplinary (scientific) and organizational personnel maximizes the probability that both types of creativity will be included in the final list of solution components. In addition, having "in-house" staff present provides a check to ensure that the solution components are relevant to the problem elements which are the focal point of the planning endeavor.

Finally, the fact that a number of external multidisciplinary experts and multiagency representatives contributed to and endorsed the proposed solution program lends legitimacy and objectivity to the program and increases its acceptability. Further, the scientific and professional composition of the group helps to cast the solution components in appropriate social science or physical science terminology, so that the recommendations are technically up to date.

Summary

The NGT solution exploration format is a deliberate, structured process which seeks to identify critical components of an innovative solution by means of a process which:

1) Focuses attention on the problem elements identified in earlier problem exploration.

2) Avoids building the solution framework around a particular theoretical or organizational model, but rather facilitates a new conceptual combination of solution components.

3) Incorporates both multidisciplinary and multiorganizational participation.

4) Calls attention to both existing and untapped resources relating to solution components.

5) Provides an aura of objectivity and legitimacy to the selected solution components due to the composition of the group.

PROPOSAL REVIEW

Many planners, once solution components have been identified, tend to proceed immediately to writing a detailed proposal. Indeed, many planners see writing a detailed proposal as the essence of planning, and the *selling* of the written proposal as an essential political process in gaining acceptance of innovations. Experience as well as research indicates this is a poorly conceived strategy.

Klein (1967) describes resistance to programs as often being a function of the way change is introduced. He notes that most planners run into trouble when the agents of change have incorporated their plans into a detailed proposal before introducing their ideas to those who will be affected and who control resources. When this happens:

". . . the innovators (writers) have usually developed a considerable investment in their plans and are often far more committed to defending them than to attempting to understand objections to them. They are not prepared to repeat with newcomers the long process . . . which finally led them to their conclusions."

Klein goes on to note that attention to critics of an innovative proposal can serve three useful functions:

"First, critics are most likely to perceive and point out any real threats to the well being of the system which may be unanticipated consequences of the projected changes. Second, they are especially likely to react against any change that might reduce the integrity of the system. Third, they are sensitive to any indication that those seeking to produce change fail to understand or identify with core values of the system they seek to influence."

Variables affecting proposal review

Early review of *preliminary* proposals by resource controllers, administrators, and opinion leaders, then, should precede the development of detailed and refined documents (Delbecq and Van de Ven, 1971). In support of this position, a number of additional insights from observations of such proposal review meetings can be added to Klein's observations. These observations can be summarized under the following list of variables affecting proposal review:

1) The format of the preliminary proposal document.
2) The composition of the reviewing body.
3) The interpersonal dynamics of review meetings.
4) The degree of support provided to the proponents of the proposal.

Preliminary proposal document • The longer and more dense the prose of a preliminary proposal document, the greater the potential for misunderstanding and "nit-picking" by reviewers. Prosaic exposition increases the tendency for sidetracked discussions focusing on semantics rather than critical aspects of the proposal. Since reviewers are not normally *technically* involved in the proposal program, a format is needed which does not obscure essential concerns with unnecessary technical details.

The more successful proposal documents leading to constructive review are essentially in outline form (i.e., clearly an early draft) and organized so as to emphasize visually the essential features to which the proposal proponents want reviewers to react. An excellent simple guide is an outline form which relies on sentences and brief phrases and which contains the following major categories: (1) a review of the sequential steps in the development of the proposal, and a list of key participants in each step; (2) a list of problem elements generated in the problem exploration phase toward which the solution program is aimed; and (3) the recommended program of action summarized in terms of solution components.

A clearly "early draft" outline document has additional benefits. First, it visually reassures reviewers that they are indeed being involved and their ideas being sought at an early stage, rather than being sold a final document. Second, the outline format makes the interjection or removal of items easy, whereas adjustments to paragraphs and sections of prosaic documents are more complex. Third, the preparation of an outline document takes much less staff energy. If the purpose of the document is really to accommodate modifications which strengthen the proposal, then expending great amounts of energy on a document which will have to be rewritten is a wasted effort. Finally, since the draft is clearly tentative, staff are less resistant to making changes than they would be if they had slaved over the document for weeks prior to the meeting.

In conclusion, an outline format presenting: (1) a preface reviewing the process and key groups involved in problem exploration and solution exploration; (2) the key problem elements being focused upon; and (3) the key solution components being proposed, is probably the most efficient format for a preliminary proposal document. Such a format facilitates the essential objectives of preliminary review—exposition, modification, and involvement.

Composition of the reviewing body • A second key concern in the process of proposal review is the composition of the reviewing group. Preliminary proposal review should be differentiated from formal review and contract signing. The individuals involved in the latter process are normally defined by official positions and roles. By contrast, preliminary proposal review aims at bringing together a group who can modify and refine the proposal, legitimate the proposal, and create a constituency to support the proposal. This generally requires a somewhat different composition.

Group composition in preliminary review should include: key administrators who will be affected by the proposed program; resource controllers who will have to approve allocation of funds or other resources (both internal budgetary officers and outside funding representatives); opinion leaders from the professional elites embedded in existing and more traditional programs; consumer representatives from problem exploration meetings; and knowledge experts from solution exploration meetings. Why this composition?

The rationale for including key administrators and budget or resource controllers is sufficiently obvious as to require no comment. The reasons for including the last three categories of representatives, however, deserve a few words of elaboration. A main source of criticism which undermines change proposals is often the professional opinion leaders from existing programs not directly involved in the innovative developmental endeavor. This potential criticism can arise in one of two ways: (1) administrators often pass on proposal documents to trusted opinion leaders for their comment, after a review meeting where the professionals were not present, in which case they make their judgments to administrators without the benefit of clarification which took place in the review meeting; or (2) professionals will be naturally cautious and feel somewhat competitive concerning any new program which is a potential source of competition and will criticize on the "grapevine" if not formally involved in review. For both reasons, confronting this important reference group directly in the proposal review process is desirable.

Representatives from the target consumer groups who took part in problem exploration meetings should be present to reaffirm the nature of the problem elements, and to provide some countervailing power against potential distortion of the solution components that may decrease their impact on priority problem concerns. Knowledge experts from the solution exploration meeting can lend an air of objectivity, and can assist in explaining technical or scientific dimensions of the solution components. Having these client and technical experts present also takes part of the burden of representing the proposal off the staff, and increases the number of communicators in the presentation of the proposed program.

Dynamics of the review meeting • A third concern is the typical ebb and flow of interaction at a proposal review meeting. Individuals invited to a review meeting tend to see their role as critics (and not necessarily friendly critics), while staff who have prepared the proposal tend to see their role as defendants. To the extent that reviewers are prepared by reading the documents before the meeting, early discussion in the meeting often concentrates on negative feedback. This sets a tone for the meeting of scapegoating the proposal, with staff becoming increasingly defensive. Soon the room separates into aggressors and defenders. As the tone of criticism picks up, reviewers see status attached to lively and trenchant criticism. As the result of this focus, the flow of negative information outweighs the flow of positive information. Presenters of the proposal leave the meeting feeling they have faced a hostile audience, and reviewers feel the proposal could not have been too strong in light of the number of criticisms raised.

Following the meeting, staff find it hard to enthusiastically undertake the rewriting of the proposal to incorporate modifications.

Many of the recommendations suggest lines of approach which are not familiar or comfortable to staff members. As the result of these dynamics, staff often approach review meetings with the enthusiasm of graduate students approaching examinations.

Degree of support provided to proponents • A final concern is the psychological impact review processes have on staff who have prepared the proposal. It is worth noting that the meeting dynamics described above do not focus on support for proposal proponents, but rather are largely an ego-deflating experience for them. The degree of ego deflation and the extent of "felt" lack of support is often proportional to the rigor and value of suggested modifications. A review process which is careless and results in no changes often seems a "supportive" experience to staff, while meetings resulting in substantial but valuable modifications often feel like defeats. Review meetings are seen by staff as leading to additional hard work, engaged in only to placate "outsiders" to the developmental endeavor.

An NGT format for proposal review

Having all too frequently experienced proposal review sessions subject to the painful dynamics just discussed, the authors have developed an NGT proposal review format which aims at ameliorating some of these difficulties. As with all NGT situations, however, a good process is no substitute for the right group composition. The format below assumes that the guidelines discussed above in terms of composition of the review body have been acted upon.

The format can be summarized as follows:

1) Prepare a preliminary proposal document in the following form:
   a. a preface which outlines the steps followed and key individuals involved in problem exploration and solution exploration.
   b. a statement of key problem elements to which the proposal seeks solutions.
   c. an outline of key solution components included in the proposed developmental program.
2) Have staff verbally review and answer questions clarifying the preliminary proposal document.
3) Present the administrators, resource controllers, consum-

ers, and experts with the NGT Preliminary Proposal Review Worksheet (Figure 5–6).

4) Allow the group to silently generate items under the headings: *Strengths of the Proposal, Modifications Which Would Improve the Proposal,* and *Sources of Assistance.*

5) Follow the normal NGT process of discussing, ranking, and rating the first two categories, *strengths* and *modifications.*

Like all NGT meetings, the meeting begins with a verbal definition of roles. In the role definition, the leader must provide a setting which encourages the development of modifications, but acknowledges the strengths of the proposal. A typical statement would be as follows:

> "We are here to review a staff document which presents a preliminary proposal for a new postgraduate education program. The document is preliminary in the sense that it is still very much open to modifications which will improve the document, but not entirely preliminary in the sense that careful prior steps have been taken in building the proposal. Mr. Smith has just reviewed the prior steps followed, and has explained the meaning of individual items in both the problem and solution categories of the proposal.

FIGURE 5–6.   Preliminary Proposal Review Worksheet.

[Strengths of the Proposal]	[Modifications Which Would Improve the Proposal]	[Sources of Assistance]
1.		
2.		
3.		
4.		
5.		
6.		
7.		
8.		
9.		
10.		

"Our purpose tonight is to appraise the adequacy of the proposal by testing the extent to which the recommended solution components constitute a program which will solve the underlying problems. It is important that we receive two different types of feedback from each of you.

[The leader hands out the NGT worksheets]

"First, we need to know those features of the proposal which you consider *strengths*. Second, we need to know what *modifications* could be made which would make this program even stronger. Finally, where we suggest modifications, we need to know where we can obtain help in building on such modifications.

[The leader then exemplifies each of the three categories on the NGT worksheet]

"Finally, let me say we are here tonight neither as critics of the proposal, nor as defenders. We are here to make sure that the solution components contained in the proposal represent the best possible thinking of this entire group. We are here, then, as *colleagues*, to refine and improve prior to taking formal action at a later time."

The meeting then proceeds in the usual NGT manner. Members of the group complete their worksheets independently, the group lists items under each category on flip charts (starting with strengths), discusses and clarifies each item, and then votes: first on strengths, then on modifications. Discussion of the vote and a final vote follow.

Special advantages of NGT

The above NGT format was developed to cope with the negative dynamics of proposal review meetings discussed above. Having group members generate and list strengths as the first step of the meeting avoids simply focusing upon criticisms of the proposal. Further, by listing strengths first, the staff receives both ego-reinforcement and assurance that the group acknowledges the positive features of the proposal before going on to suggest modifications.

Listing and discussing strengths, however, is not merely a matter of reinforcing staff and creating a positive atmosphere. Often the trade-offs between the strengths of the suggested program of action and the strengths of modifications are not so obvious. For example, in reviewing a proposal of an experimental study, the strength of a proposed design which incorporates many aspects of the real world must often be weighed against the value of a modification which would provide better control. Normally, the staff presenting the proposal has weighed these matters, and arrived at a judgment that the advantages of realism outweigh the advantages of tighter control.

The juxtaposition of strengths and modifications, then, has two advantages: (1) it highlights trade-offs or costs of modifications so the group is careful in tampering with proposed solution components; and (2) it places group members in the position of defending noted strengths so that the staff are not the sole articulators of the advantages of the present design.

The wording of the second worksheet category, *Modifications Which Would Improve the Proposal,* was not arrived at easily. There are two features of this wording worth noting. The first and obvious point is the accentuation of the positive. This is a more positive wording than "weaknesses," "criticisms," "negative aspects," etc. A second feature, however, is more substantive. The category asks the participant who sees a weakness to suggest a solution to the weakness, not simply to point it out. The third category (*Sources of Assistance*) goes further and asks the individual suggesting the modification to also suggest resources who could help staff accomplish the modification. Often staff resistance is based less on refusal to recognize the justification for the modification than on a feeling of not knowing how to implement the modification. By approaching criticism in this fashion, the NGT format is both less threatening to staff and more challenging to reviewers who must provide helpful suggestions rather than merely criticize.

The NGT format often increases the sense of involvement by reviewers as well. An individual who suggests a modification will often volunteer to help proposal proponents or refer them to a source of assistance. This is a viable form of low-key cooperation.

Finally, as in other NGT meetings, the voting procedure is very important. A high-status, aggressive, articulate critic who is suggesting a modification about which he feels strongly, but which the other evaluators appraise as less strategic, is not allowed to control the group and impose modifications which will not truly strengthen the proposal.

The NGT meeting, however, is not intended to fend off modifications. Success in gaining acceptance of and emotional identification with the proposal, as well as improving the proposal, depends on the ability of the group to truly modify and change the preliminary document. Here, the NGT leader can be of great help.

Preferably, in a proposal review meeting the leader should not be a staff member who participated in the evolution of the proposal. A leader who is clearly neutral is best. On the other hand, staff concerns are well represented, since the NGT format and the suggested group composition ensure that staff, consumers, and knowledge experts are able to articulate strengths, as well as creatively explore modifications, as full participants along with reviewers.

Of the many utilizations of NGT in planning situations, this particular format is one of the most interesting. Planners confronted with controversial proposals will find the format extremely helpful in directing a potentially destructive situation into one which constructively accentuates the strengths of the proposal as well as facilitates modification.

Summary

The NGT preliminary proposal review format is a structured meeting which accomplishes the following purposes: (1) brings together administrators, resource controllers, professional opinion leaders, consumer representatives, outside experts, and staff to review a proposal at an early phase, wherein proponents of a proposal are still open to suggested changes; (2) facilitates the incorporation of modifications that would improve the proposal and increase its acceptability; (3) focuses upon an outline document which contains the essential features of the proposal; (4) provides an atmosphere of collegiality rather than a separation of roles into critics and defenders; (5) ensures that the positive features of the proposal are emphasized in the meeting along with modifications; and (6) elicits suggestions for modifications in a manner which incorporates sources for assistance in carrying out the changes.

CONCLUSION

This chapter has focused upon several specific applications of NGT to planning situations. Several important themes have been recurrent in the discussion of the applications: group composition, verbal role definitions, and carefully worded NGT questions or worksheets. The four uses discussed (exploratory research, citizen participation, utilization of multidisciplinary experts, and proposal review) are by no means the only applications of NGT in planning. They are, however, key applications to which we have applied the technique in planning situations in health, education, welfare, and project management.

We could go on and document other applications: priority setting, development of research designs, budget review, etc. However, to do so would limit the creativity and tax the interest of the reader. Rather, we hope that this chapter, by illustrating specific applications of NGT, will suggest the utility of the technique in major organizational and planning concerns. Chapter 3, together with these illustrations, should unlock the reader's imagination in adapting NGT dynamics to other meeting settings.

As suggested at the beginning of the chapter, Delphi can also be used in similar situations. Delphi has often been employed as a technique for involving multidisciplinary experts in planning. Chapter 4 should help the reader understand how to use Delphi in lieu of NGT where groups cannot be brought together physically for a meeting.

It is our hope that this book will help you consider the technique for many applications beyond those we have illustrated, and that you will be able to do so with skill and success.

REFERENCES

Campbell, A. A. "Two Problems in the Use of the Open Question." *Journal of Abnormal and Social Psychology,* 40 (1945): 340–43.

Crutchfield, R. S., and D. A. Gordon. "Variations in Respondents' Interpretations on an Opinion-pool Question." *International Journal of Opinion and Attitude Research,* 1, 3 (1947): 1–12.

Dalton, Gene W. "Influence and Organization Change." Paper presented at the CARI Conference on Organization Behavior Models, Kent State University, 1969.

Dean, L. R. "Interaction Reported and Observed: The Case of One Local Union." *Human Organization,* 17, 3 (1958): 36–44.

Delbecq, A. L. "How Informal Organization Evolves: Interpersonal Choice and Subgroup Formation." In *Contemporary Readings in Organizational Behavior.* F. Luthans, ed. McGraw-Hill, 1972.

Delbecq, A. L., and A. H. Van de Ven. "A Group Process Model for Problem Identification and Program Planning." *Journal of Applied Behavioral Science,* 7, 4 (July–August 1971).

Delbecq, A. L., and A. H. Van de Ven. "The Nominal Group as a Pilot Research Instrument." *American Journal of Public Health* (March 1972).

Delbecq, A. L., A. H. Van de Ven, and R. Wallace. "Critical Problems in Health Planning: Potential Management Contributions." Paper presented at 32nd Annual Meeting of Academy of Management, August 13–16, 1972.

Flanagan, J. C. "The Critical Incident Technique." *Psychological Bulletin*, 51 (1954): 327–58.

Gordan, Gerald, and Edward Morse. "Creative Potential and Organization Structure." Proceedings of the 28th Annual Meeting of the Academy of Management, Chicago, Illinois, December 1968.

Guilford, J. P. *Psychometric Methods*. McGraw-Hill, 1954.

Hage, Jerald. *Techniques and Problems of Theory Construction*. Unpublished paper, University of Wisconsin, Madison, 1971.

Heller, F. A. "Group Feedback Analysis: A Method of Field Research." *Psychological Bulletin*, 72, 2 (1969): 108–17.

Hoffman, L. R. "Group Problem Solving." In *Advances in Experimental Social Psychology*, Pt. II. L. Berkowitz, ed. Academic Press, 1965.

Hoffman, L. R., and N. R. F. Maier. "Quality and Acceptance of Problem Solutions by Members of Homogeneous and Heterogeneous Groups." *Journal of Abnormal and Social Psychology*, 62 (1961).

Hoffman, L. R. and G. G. Smith. "Some Factors Affecting the Behavior of Members of Problem-Solving Groups." *Sociometry*, 23 (1960): 273–91.

Jahoda, M., M. Deutsch, and S. Cook. *Research Methods in Social Relations*. Dryden Press, 1951.

Klein, D. C. "Some Notes on the Dynamics of Resistance to Change: The Defender Role." In *Concepts for Social Change*. G. Watson, ed. Cooperative Project for Educational Development, National Training Laboratories, NEA, 1967.

Lipsky, M. "Protest as a Political Resource." Discussion paper, Institute for Research on Poverty, University of Wisconsin, Madison, 1971.

Merton, R. K. and P. L. Kendall. "The Focused Interview." *American Journal of Sociology*, 51 (1946): 541–57.

Muscio, B. "The Influence of the Form of a Question." *British Journal of Psychology*, 8 (1916): 351–86.

Nunnally, J. C. *Psychometric Theory*. McGraw-Hill, 1968.

Payne, S. L. *The Art of Asking Questions.* Princeton University Press, 1951.

Science Policy Research Unit. "Success and Failure in Industrial Innovation." Report on Project Sappho, University of Sussex Center for the Study of Industrial Innovation, 1972.

Smet, J. A. "A Study of the Critical Requirements for Instructors of General Psychology Courses." *University of Pittsburgh Bulletin,* 48 (1952): 279–84.

Speak, M. "Communication Failure in Questioning: Errors, Misrepresentations and Personal Frames of Reference." *Occupational Psychology,* 41 (1967): 169–79.

Thorndike, R. L. and G. H. Gallup. "Verbal Intelligence in the American Adult." *Journal of General Psychology,* 30 (1944): 75–85.

Toffler, Alvin. *Future Shock.* Random House, 1970.

Utterback, James. "The Process of Technological Innovations Within the Firm." *Academy of Management Journal,* 14, 1 (March 1971): 75–88.

Van de Ven, A. H., and A. L. Delbecq. "Nominal versus Interacting Group Processes for Committee Decision-Making Effectiveness." *Academy of Management Journal,* 14, 3 (1971).

Wagner, R. F. "A Study of Critical Requirements for Dentists." *University of Pittsburgh Bulletin,* 46 (1950): 331–39.

Weitz, J. "Verbal and Pictorial Questionnaires in Market Research." *Journal of Applied Psychology,* 34 (1950): 363–66.

Wells, W. D. "How Chronic Overclaimers Distort Survey Findings." *Journal of Advertising Research,* 3, 2 (1963): 8–18.

Appendix

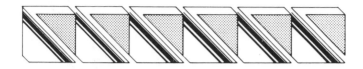

SCHOOL OF NURSING OF THE
UNIVERSITY OF WISCONSIN, MADISON
PROJECT: REALIGNMENT OF ROLES IN NURSING

DELPHI QUESTIONNAIRE #1

Instructions for responding to Delphi Questionnaire #1:

Please read all questions before responding.

Under each question of this Delphi there are two columns. The left-hand column is entitled "Responsibilities." Under this column, please list the responsibilities you expect the nurse to *add* or *give up* in the next ten years. The question itself will tell you which way to respond.

The right-hand column is entitled "Examples." It is *very important that you give an example* corresponding to *each* of your opinions in the left-hand column. The example should be *brief* but should demonstrate why it is important to add or give up that specific responsibility. The answers in both columns will give us two ways of viewing your answers to be sure we do not misinterpret your responses.

Please have the completed questionnaire in the mail to us by ___(date)___ . A self-addressed, stamped envelope has been enclosed for your convenience.

QUESTIONNAIRE #1(a)

Code _____   Date _____

1. Think about the professional nurse delivering *outpatient* (*ambulatory*) health care.

A. What is the professional nurse responsible for today that such a person *should not* be generally responsible for ten years from now? In each case, provide a brief example, possibly from your own experience, that leads you to believe that this is an important and desirable change.

Responsibilities	Examples
1. Management	a. scheduling patients b. scheduling M.D. and R.N. time c. ordering drugs and supplies d. clerical functions
2. Simple treatment and auxiliary services	a. preparing for minor surgical procedures b. chaperone pelvics, etc. c. provide treatments (apply bandages, etc.) d. make arrangements for follow-up care, referrals, or hospital admissions

QUESTIONNAIRE: #1(b)

Code _____ Date _____

B. What *should* that professional nurse be responsible for ten years from now that such a person is not generally responsible for today? In each case, provide a brief example, possibly from your own experience, that leads you to believe that this is an important and desirable change. (This question also refers to outpatient/ambulatory care.)

Responsibilities	Examples
1. Total assessment of diagnostic and therapeutic needs of patients	a. Complete work-ups b. history taking c. management d. education
2. Ambulatory chronic disease management	all aspects of care
3. Acute disease management	a. assessment b. work-up c. management
4. Perform complex procedures	spinal taps, etc.

DELPHI QUESTIONNAIRE #2

Instructions for responding to Delphi Questionnaire #2:

We have listed on a separate page the responses to the questions from the first Delphi mailing. Please do three things to these lists:

1) Review all items on each list. Comment, in one or two statements, on any item(s) you wish. You may argue in favor of an item, or request clarification. Brevity and clarity will facilitate analysis.

2) Select the seven responsibilities that you feel are the most important to add (delete) from the nursing role. Assign the value seven (7) to the responsibility you feel is most important: (a) to add to the professional nurse's responsibilities; or (b) to delete from the professional nurse's responsibilities, as identified in the stem of the statement. Assign six (6) to the next most important and so on until the seventh item (the least important of the seven) is assigned a value of one (1). Remember that 7 should be assigned to the responsibility you feel is *most important* to add or delete. Note: This is merely a preliminary vote. It is not binding.

3) Return your response in the enclosed self-addressed, stamped envelope by
      (date)
   _____

QUESTIONNAIRE #2(a)

Code _____   Date _____

Remember: 1. Choose only seven items.
          2. Give weight of "7" to the most important, "6" to the second
             most, etc.

Vote	Responsibilities	Comment
	In ten years nurses in an *outpatient/ambulatory* setting *will be* generally responsible for:	
	1. *screening* healthy population	
6	2. *assessing patient's need* for medical treatment and health care through the use of histories, physical examinations, lab tests, and x-rays.	
	3. *referring patients* to MDs when the nurse feels it is appropriate.	*seems not a responsibility but outgrowth of working together*
	4. *diagnostic and treatment procedures* such as lumbar puncture, paracentesis, and suturing wounds.	
5	5. *treating simple* acute illness *conditions* including prescribing symptomatic treatment.	
	6. providing *emergency care.*	
2	7. medical *management of* the stabilized *chronically ill* including adjusting medication regime when indicated.	
	8. *physical comfort* and support of patient.	
	9. *referral* of patients to other health professionals and agencies when indicated.	

QUESTIONNAIRE #2(a)
(con't)

Vote	Responsibilities	Comment
	10. making *home visits* for follow-up care which includes evaluating and adjusting the medical treatment plan.	
4	11. *assuming leadership* for coordinating the activities of multidisciplinary *health care team members.*	
	12. *teaching and counseling* patients and families.	
	13. developing and conducting *community health education* programs.	must relate education to care process; not separate
	14. *teaching* of other *health care providers.*	
1	15. systematic *recording* of patient data.	
	16. identification of *community health* problems and establishment of nursing services to meet these needs.	
	17. participating in efforts to improve *health services* on the national, state, and local levels.	extracurricular
	18. *evaluating* the *quality and effectiveness* of nursing service (e.g., cost/benefit analysis, etc.).	don't separate from rest of system
	19. conducting *research* to solve nurse care problems and develop nursing theory.	
	20. establishing a system of *peer review* and setting up *standards* or criteria for	why not standards that apply to problem, not professional?

QUESTIONNAIRE #2(a)
(con't)

Vote	Responsibilities	Comment
	levels of practice within nursing.	
___	21. establishing *nursing* as an *independent* source of health care delivery.	*violently negative !*
7	22. *joint decision making* on a nurse-physician health-care delivery team.	
___	23. identifying *nursing needs* of patients.	
___	24. acting as the *patient's* advocate.	*Can't - she's a provider; contradiction in terms*
___	25. *admitting and discharging* patients in health-care institutions.	
3	26. *psychological* support of patients.	

QUESTIONNAIRE #2(b)

Code _____   Date _____

Remember: 1. Choose only seven items.
               2. Give weight of "7" to the most important, "6" to the second most, etc.

Vote	Responsibilities	Comment
	In ten years nurses in an *outpatient/ambulatory* setting will *not* generally be responsible for:	
7	1. *housekeeping tasks* such as cleaning equipment and examining rooms.	This section was difficult for me
2	2. maintaining, ordering, and purchasing *supplies* and *equipment*.	because I find only 7 items the role model
6	3. *supervision of support personnel* (clerical, housekeeping, etc.)	I see should even remotely be doing.
	4. *scheduling* of examining rooms and assigning space to physicians and other personnel.	The order of the remaining 14 items to
5	5. *escorting and transporting patients* to various departments and services.	be deleted seems less relevant since
	6. *locating* physicians or patients.	they all should go,
	7. *obtaining information* (lab reports, x-rays, etc.) for the physician.	to enable the nurse to be the primary
3	8. *receptionist activities* (e.g., telephone, making appointments, etc.).	provider.
4	9. *routine record keeping* such as bookkeeping, billing, insurance forms, and fee collection.	

QUESTIONNAIRE #2(b)
(con't)

Vote		Responsibilities	Comment
_____	10.	filling out of *forms to obtain* various *services*.	
_____	11.	*routine screening procedures* such as vision and hearing tests, EKG, pulmonary functions, etc.	
_____	12.	routine *history* and *physical examination*.	
_____	13.	*routine treatments* such as: dressings, injections, catheter changes, etc.	
_____	14.	*first aid* and emergency treatment.	
_____	15.	*assisting* MD with technical procedures and treatments.	
_/___	16.	*assisting* MD with the *physical examination*, e.g., preparing and chaperoning patient for pelvic exam.	
_____	17.	family *counseling*.	
_____	18.	*interpreting* and explaining *doctor's orders*.	
_____	19.	follow up on *test results* and missed *visits*.	
_____	20.	routine *home care*.	
_____	21.	handling *patient complaints*.	

DELPHI QUESTIONNAIRE #3

Instructions for responding to Delphi Questionnaire #3:

BACKGROUND

The enclosed questionnaire contains:

1) participants' statements of responsibilities the nurse will have or give up in ten years in both an outpatient/ambulatory and inpatient setting.
2) a preliminary ranking of these responsibilities by the participants.
3) comments given on each responsibility.

The first column lists the vote for each responsibility listed in the second column. The third column contains a summary of the comments made for each responsibility. A fourth column, entitled Implications and Reactions, is provided for you to influence the final vote and suggest implications for future action.

TASK

Comment on any item(s) you wish so as to: clarify its meaning, influence its ranking in the final vote, and/or suggest implications for future action. For those responsibilities that you wish to comment upon, please limit yourselves to no more than three short and precise statements.

QUESTIONNAIRE #3(a)

Code _____ Date _____

In ten years, nurses in an outpatient/ambulatory setting will *not* generally be responsible for:

Vote	Responsibilities	Comments	Implications and Reactions
466	*housekeeping tasks* such as cleaning equipment and examining rooms.	a) This is a waste of the nurse's time. b) Return responsibility for delicate equipment and when there is a danger of infection. c) Task should be assumed by managerial personnel.	In many facilities these tasks have already been eliminated.
342	*routine record keeping* such as book-keeping, billing, insurance forms, and fee collection.	a) Not a nursing responsibility, requires no nursing knowledge. b) Machines should do this.	
284	maintaining, ordering, and purchasing *supplies and equipment.*	a) This is a waste of the nurse's time. Only when decisions are involved, e.g., kind of equipment to purchase, determining procedure for maintenance. b) c) Task should be assumed by managerial personnel.	Space should be assigned mutually and systematically by Registering/Assigning personnel.
219	*scheduling* of examining rooms and assigning space to physicians and other personnel.	a) This is a waste of nursing time, requires no nursing knowledge. b) Automatic scheduling is a necessity. c) Ancillary personnel can do this, e.g., managerial personnel. d) Could be important to patients as the nurse is most aware of problems here. e) If the assignment involves the nurse, then she needs to have input into the decision.	

QUESTIONNAIRE #3(a)
(con't)

Code _____

Date _____

In ten years, nurses in an outpatient/ambulatory setting will *not* generally be responsible for:

Vote	Responsibilities		Comments	Implications and Reactions
218	*receptionist activities* (e.g., telephone, making appointments, etc.).	a)	This is a waste of nursing time.	*managerial responsibility*
		b)	Nurses may need to supervise the receptionist.	
		c)	Ancillary personnel can do this.	
		d)	Opportunity for professional judgment and decisions may arise.	
		e)	Needs clarification: much valid care and information can be handled by phone.	
193	*escorting and transporting patients* to various departments and services.	a)	This is a waste of nursing time and talent.	*Another routine administrative task, non-nursing except in selected instances*
		b)	Could be important because judgment about the status of the patient may be necessary.	
		c)	Important when patient is seriously ill.	
		d)	Ancillary personnel can do this.	
		e)	Can be most important and needed demonstration of caring.	
120	*supervision of support personnel* (clerical, housekeeping, etc.).	a)	This is not a nursing responsibility.	*(a) and (d)*
		b)	Needs clarification, e.g., some nursing knowledge may be needed.	
		c)	Who else can do it in a meaningful way?	

Vote	Responsibilities	Comments	Implications and Reactions
		d) Task should be assumed by managerial personnel.	
		e) Need clarification: e.g., I might not supervise housekeeping but I need to help them understand cleanliness and manner in which cleaning is done.	
110	locating physicians or patients.	a) This is a waste of nursing time and talent.	*(d)*
		b) Ancillary personnel can do this.	
		c) Nurse may locate patient if patient is to see nurse.	
		d) May be important in a given situation.	
94	filling out of forms to obtain various services.	a) This is not a nursing responsibility.	*I agree with (d) but would add that routine referrals should be clerical task*
		b) Ancillary personnel can do this, e.g., clerks, aides.	
		c) Clarification needed: is this different from identifying the content which justifies the service, e.g., data for patient referral?	
		d) Depends upon the type of forms: e.g., nurses will fill out some and physicians will fill out others.	
		e) This is a logical step after *the nurse* decides what services are needed.	
78	obtaining information (lab reports, x-rays, etc.) for the physician.	a) This is not a nursing responsibility.	*routinely (a) but (d) in selected instances*
		b) Ancillary personnel can do this, e.g., clerks or telephone operators.	
		c) The nurse can obtain it for herself.	
		d) May be necessary for the nurse to do this in emergency situations.	

QUESTIONNAIRE #3(a)
(con't)

Code _____   Date _____

In ten years, nurses in an outpatient/ambulatory setting will *not* generally be responsible for:

Vote	Responsibilities	Comments	Implications and Reactions
17	family *counseling*.	a) Think will be part of nursing role included in health teaching. b) Who else would do this? c) Is an essential activity for nursing.	*(e)*
16	routine *history* and *physical examination*.	a) Requires procedural or technical knowledge—not necessarily decisions or judgment. b) Ancillary personnel can do it, e.g., admission clerks. c) Is part of responsibility for giving health care. d) "Routine" aspect is never apparent until completed. e) Now being done—an important but not major contribution to health care. f) If just routine screening, nurse will not be responsible so depends on your rationale. g) Clarify "routine"—does this mean considerable time spent in activity? h) Delete now and in future. i) Will be a nursing function.	*(e), therefore (f) and (i) follow logically*
13	*assisting MD with the physical examination*, e.g., preparing and chaperoning patient for pelvic exam.	a) Is important for support of patient. b) Not needed except in special situations. c) Assume this means the goal of the nurse is to meet physician's needs—if so disagree with role. d) Done by LPN and technicians in nurse settings now. e) Opportunity for nursing judgments	*(f)*

QUESTIONNAIRE #3(b)

Code _____   Date _____

In ten years nurses in an outpatient/ambulatory setting *will be* generally responsible for:

Vote	Responsibilities	Comments	Implications and Reactions
309	*assessing patient's need* for medical treatment and health care through the use of histories, physical examinations, lab tests, and x-rays.	a) Government will force this function on nurses. b) This is already going on at Cumberland, Maryland. c) This is an MD's responsibility. d) What about assessment using other tools or methods? e) Nurses should assess much more than physical needs. f) Nurses are best qualified for this. g) Yes, but nurses will need more training first.	agree completely with statement and (g)
243.5	medical *management of* the stabilized chronically ill including adjusting medication regime when indicated.	a) Nurses do this now. b) This should include psychosocial management. c) P.A. should do this. d) Nurses should have their own caseload. e) "Nursing" *not* medical management.	agree with item and (f)
177.5	*treating simple* acute illness *conditions* including prescribing symptomatic treatment.	a) What is a simple acute illness? b) This is a must. c) Better done by a technician or P.A. d) You'll have to prove you can do it! e) This would be great in school nursing.	agree but assume careful delineation of conditions covered

QUESTIONNAIRE #3(b)
(con't)

Code _____   Date _____

In ten years nurses in an outpatient/ambulatory setting *will be* generally responsible for:

Vote	Responsibilities	Comments	Implications and Reactions
175	teaching and counseling patients and families.	a) This is part of nurse role now! b) Community workers can do this! c) Patients will be deciding what information they need to make their own decision.	(a)
134	joint decision making on a nurse-physician health-care delivery team.	a) There is more than nurse and physician on a health team? b) Being done more and more.	completely agree
114	assuming leadership for coordinating the activities of multidisciplinary health-care team members.	a) What is meant by coordinating? b) This should include community health teams. c) This is being done now in some places. d) Should not be done in a general sense. e) No! Administration should handle this.	agree in general but pattern should include flexibility within team
112	making home visits for follow-up care which includes evaluating and adjusting the medical treatment plan.	a) Nurses already doing this and doctors won't. b) This is expensive but valuable. c) Nurses don't adjust treatment now. d) This is a poor use of nurse's time.	(a) - is a primary nursing function
112	identification of community health problems and establishment of nursing services to meet these needs.	a) Do this on team basis. b) Should be doing now.	agree but curriculum must be developed

Vote	Responsibilities	Comments	Implications and Reactions
99	*screening* healthy population.	a) What populations? b) Not clear what is included. Do this eyeball to eyeball or mass screening? c) Would waste time of the nurse. No health professional should screen; use technicians or machines. d) Yes, this provides a good opportunity for teaching and counseling.	*statement needs clarification*
98	identifying *nursing needs* of patients.	a) Should be principally responsible for health maintenance aspects. b) Nurses do it now. c) Should also provide needed care.	*agree; also plan and evaluate effects of care*
89.5	*referring patients* to MDs when the nurse feels it is appropriate.	a) Yes! b) Should not be permitted to refer patients to *new* specialists. c) So what's new?	*is already appropriate nursing role*
74	establishing *nursing* as an *independent* source of health care delivery.	a) No provider should be independent of other providers. b) "Why is nursing so hung up on this?" c) This will fractionate the health system. d) No hope for this. e) No!! f) What does this mean? g) Nurses should not be servants of physicians.	*a distinct possibility which needs to be tested*
72	participating in efforts to improve *health services* on the national, state, and local levels.	a) Government will do this. b) Too general. c) Doing now. d) Will not be a widespread trend.	*has been happening since 1933*
68	acting as the *patients' advocate.*	a) Nurse should not be an ombudsman.	*hopefully will learn to be*

QUESTIONNAIRE #3(b)
(con't)

Code _____   Date _____

In ten years nurses in an outpatient/ambulatory setting *will be* generally responsible for:

Vote	Responsibilities		Comments	Implications and Reactions
63	establishing a system of *peer review* and setting up *standards* or criteria for levels of practice within nursing.	a)	Doing this now.	agree with (f) and (a), in that some progress is being made in this direction
		b)	Need criteria for evaluation.	
		c)	Role of ANA.	
		d)	Peer review is on the way out.	
		e)	Criteria should be same for all providers.	
		f)	Very important.	
58	developing and conducting *community health education* programs.	a)	Being done now.	
		b)	Health educators should do this.	
		c)	Someone else will do this.	
58	conducting *research* to solve nurse care problems and develop nursing theory.	a)	Typical nurse is not qualified.	
		b)	Can't do both research and develop theory.	
		c)	We have more important things to do.	
54	providing *emergency care*.	a)	Only in remote areas and then need training.	selectively and only with specialized training
		b)	Ancillary personnel can do this.	
		c)	We already have nurses who are traumatologists.	
43.5	*referral* of patients to other health professionals and agencies when indicated.	a)	Nurses already doing this.	(a)
38	evaluating the *quality and effectiveness* of nursing service (e.g., cost/benefit analysis, etc.)	a)	ANA should do this.	agree with statement that curricula need to be developed to prepare nurses for these functions
		b)	Should be done only on experimental basis.	
		c)	Business manager can do this better.	
		d)	Should evaluate quality but not costs.	

DELPHI QUESTIONNAIRE #4

Instructions for responding to Delphi Questionnaire #4:

BACKGROUND

The responsibilities listed in Questionnaires #1 and #2 were put into eighteen major categories. The comments from Questionnaire #2 and the reactions from Questionnaire #3 were summarized. Potential issues for each major category were identified from these comments.

TASK

Your task is to select the seven *most important issues* you would like to have discussed at the Conference. Give a vote of seven (7) to the most important issue, six (6) to the second most important, and so on until the value of one (1) is assigned to the least important issue of the seven. A comment column is provided if you wish to use it to explain your vote or to comment on the issue. Brief, concise comments limited to one or two statements will be helpful to us as we choose the topics for part of the Conference.

Since we may have missed some important issues that you feel should be considered at the Conference on Role Realignment, please list these issues, your vote, and your arguments as to why they are appropriate on the last page of this Delphi Questionnaire.

QUESTIONNAIRE #4

Code _____ Date _____

Category	Summary of Comments from Delphi #2 & #3	Issues	Vote	Comments
Managerial, clerical, and housekeeping activities:	These are not the responsibility of the nurse, let alone the extended role nurse; in certain circumstances they could be performed by a nurse as a means for accomplishing nursing role (e.g., data collection, providing support) or for indirectly affecting patient care (e.g., teaching of ancillary personnel, providing input into policy decisions regarding activities).	1. By what means can nursing opportunities provided by these activies be otherwise provided? 2. How can the system be restructured so that these tasks can be assumed by others?	| |	
a) housekeeping tasks such as cleaning equipment and examining rooms.				
b) routine record-keeping such as bookkeeping, billing, insurance forms, and fee collection.				
c) maintaining, ordering, and purchasing supplies and equipment.				
d) scheduling of examining rooms and assigning space to physicians and other personnel.				
e) receptionist activities (e.g., telephone, making appointments, etc.).				
f) escorting and transporting patients to various departments and services.				
g) supervision of support personnel (clerical, housekeeping, etc.)				
h) locating physicians or patients.				
i) filling out of forms to obtain various services.				

QUESTIONNAIRE #4
(con't)

Code ———

Date ———

Category	Summary of Comments from Delphi #2 & #3	Issues	Vote	Comments
j) obtaining information (lab reports, x-rays, etc.) for the physician.				
k) clerical tasks (e.g., transcribing orders, filling out lab slips).				
l) providing or arranging for services of nonprofessional departments such as housekeeping, cleaning rooms, passing trays.				
m) transporting patients to appointments and running errands.				
n) receptionist tasks (e.g., directing visitors).				
o) supervising the work of personnel from other departments such as housekeeping personnel.				
p) maintaining equipment in proper working order.				
q) recording routine information on the patient's chart (e.g., insurance data).				
r) ensuring that equipment and supplies are available.				

QUESTIONNAIRE #4
(con't)

Code _____

Date _____

Category	Summary of Comments from Delphi #2 & #3	Issues	Vote	Comments
s) assuming hospital management duties (especially on evening and night shifts). t) providing or arranging for services of other professional departments such as pharmacy, x-ray. u) managing the patient unit (e.g., scheduling personnel). v) orienting non-nursing personnel to the unit.				
Assisting the physician while he is diagnosing and treating the patient (e.g., chaperoning for pelvic exam., setting up equipment): a) assisting MD with the physical examination, e.g., preparing and chaperoning patient for pelvic exam.	Assisting MDs *per se* can be performed by LPNs and technicians. In certain circumstances, however, nurses can be helpful to the patient by providing support. Also, tasks may provide an entre to the patient for collection of information.	1. Who should be responsible for supervision and/or training of those who assist physicians? 2. The support of patients and collection of information is not seen as issue.	|	
Performance of technical procedures, e.g., dressings, catheter changes, injections, lumbar punctures, IVs, paracentesis, suturing wounds, preparing medications for distribution, passing	Opinions vary markedly on these tasks. Some participants feel procedures requiring little skill should be delegated to others.	1. For which patients or populations should each of the procedures be performed by nurses?	|	

Category	Summary of Comments from Delphi #2 & #3	Issues	Vote	Comments
medications, baths, enema, IPPB, gastric intubation: a) assisting MDs with technical procedures and treatment. b) routine treatments such as: dressings, injections, catheter changes, etc. c) diagnostic and treatment procedures such as lumbar puncture, paracentesis, and suturing wounds. d) preparing medications for distribution. e) technical tasks related to patient care (e.g., baths, TPR, enema). f) passing medications (e.g., oral, intramuscular). g) administering specific therapies (such as IV and IPPB). h) prescribing and doing routine diagnostic and therapeutic procedures (e.g., gastric intubation, IV). i) doing special diagnostic and therapeutic procedures (e.g., paracentesis, minor surgery).	Some feel procedures requiring considerable skill should be the responsibility of MD or PA. Persons at various levels can be trained to perform the tasks. Whether nurses do these depends upon the purpose and implications. Nurse might perform these tasks to evaluate the patient or collect information.	2. If nurses are to increase the number of procedures which they are capable of performing, how will they get the needed training? 3. Is the performance of increasingly complex technical procedures prescribed by someone else an acceptable approach to realignment of nursing roles?		

Index

5 6-MUR-84 83 82 81 80